THE RADIANCE OF NOTHINGNESS

To the One in all, the all in One

Manish Sharma

FanatiXx® Publication

FanatiXx® Publication
Rourkela | Mumbai | Delhi NCR | Ahmedabad

The Radiance of Nothingness by Mr. Manish Sharma

ISBN: 978-93-7406-672-0

First Edition – 2025

This is an Original Work of the Author.
All works of the author's imagination.
Any resemblance to actual persons, living or dead, is purely coincidental.

For permissions, inquiries, or feedback:
Email: outreach@fanatixx.info
Instagram: @fanatixxpublication

Gratitude

To the inner guidance, the guru field, and the silence itself, which has been the greatest teacher of all.

To all who have opened doors, to all whose love has nourished me, to all whose presence has steadied my steps, and to all whose innocence and joy reflect the truth, this book is for you.

With folded hands and a heart wide with wonder, I bow to every friend, guru, seeker, and stranger who, knowingly or unknowingly, has walked with me. Some offered wisdom, others offered laughter, some challenged me, and others embraced me when I faltered. Each, in their own way, was a spark that revealed light where I thought there was none.

I bow especially to my gurus and guides, living and eternal, whose clarity, patience, and love became the bridge across the restless waters of doubt. In moments when shadows of confusion gathered thick, their words and silence reminded me that I am not the storm, but the sky itself untouched, vast, and free.

Essence of Knowledge program of my guru Tarun Pradhan Ji has taught me that knowledge is not the piling of concepts but the refinement of seeing. True knowledge is alive, tested in direct experience, guided by logic, and confirmed in direct recognition of Self. His clarity reminds me to treat knowledge not as a possession, but as a living fabric, open and ready to dissolve into wisdom.

If any passage here brings you comfort, let the gratitude flow back to the teachers, saints, seekers, and companions whose presence watered the seed. If any word points you inward, let it be their blessing reaching you through me. I owe them the courage to ask, the stillness to listen, and the laughter to walk lightly, even though the heaviest of days.

To the unseen hands that held me, to the cosmic play that carried me, and to the one Self shining as all forms, my gratitude is without end.

In deepest gratitude.

Manish Sharma

About the Author

Manish Sharma is a mentor, writer, and seeker of truth whose path has been one of listening, questioning, and dissolving into silence. Drawn to the wisdom of self-inquiry and the fragrance of non-duality, he writes not as a teacher who knows, but as a fellow traveler pointing toward what has always been here.

His words carry a simplicity that touches the heart, weaving poetry and clarity into gentle reminders of who we are beneath the noise of mind and world. He believes that truth is not hidden in distant scriptures or faraway journeys but shines quietly in the immediacy of our own awareness.

Through his writings, Manish invites readers to slow down, to breathe, to return to the stillness within, and to rediscover the wholeness that was never absent. For him, life itself is the teacher, every question, every smile, every silence, a doorway to the eternal.

The Journey Unfolds

Index

Preface

A love note to the seeker who doesn't yet know they are the sought.

This book is not meant to teach you something new. It is meant to remind you of what you already know deep within. Every chapter is a gentle nudge, a playful whisper, and sometimes a sharp knock on the door of awareness reminding you to look, really look, at what is always here.

I did not write this as a scholar or philosopher. I wrote it as a fellow traveler, someone who has stumbled, searched, laughed, meditated, and questioned. Along the way, I discovered that truth is not hidden in distant places; it shines quietly in the simplicity of our everyday experience.

The journey through these pages is not about gathering beliefs, doctrines, or rituals. It is about dissolving them. The real path is not about becoming someone, but about unlearning who you thought you were. It is not about striving toward a distant goal, but about relaxing into the fullness of the present moment.

The structure of this book mirrors the natural unfolding of knowledge:

The early chapters explore the Existence, the nature of Experience, the Experiencer and the illusions that shape our perception.

The middle chapters open into deeper insights like memory, time, and the subtle dance between experiencer and experience.

The later chapters reveal the truth of Oneness, where all divisions dissolve.

And finally, the last chapter provides simple practices, listening, contemplation, and abiding that anchor knowledge in daily life.

The style blends depth with lightness. You'll find the clarity of Advaita Vedanta alongside the playful freedom, so the words don't feel like a burden but like a song. The truth is vast, yet it is not heavy. It dances.

I invite you to read these words slowly, not as instructions but as mirrors. Pause when something touches you. Skip when something feels unclear. It may return to you later in silence. Above all, treat this book as a companion, not as a doctrine.

May these pages help you to remember what cannot be forgotten: that you are already whole, already free, already the witnessing awareness in which all of life arises.

With love and gratitude...

About Me

Spoiler: I found nothing, and that nothing was everything.

I am not a teacher, not a guru, not a scholar. I am simply a wanderer who became curious about the question that hides behind all others: "Who am I?"

Life has carried me across many landscapes; professional, relational, creative, and spiritual. In one world, I lead teams, build data strategies, and translate complexity into clarity. In another, I write, reflect, and seek silence beneath the noise. And in between, I laugh with friends, love deeply, stumble often, and rediscover wonder in the most ordinary of moments.

Each role, executive, seeker, partner, friend, seemed solid for a time, yet each dissolved when I looked closely. Titles, successes, even failures shifted like clouds in a wide sky. What remained constant was awareness itself: the silent witness behind every dashboard I designed, every meditation I sat through, every sunrise over an airport window, every conversation that opened my heart.

This book is not written from mastery, but from discovery. It is neither instruction nor doctrine, but a living diary of curiosity. Each chapter reflects my own walk, stumbling, questioning, doubting, sometimes resisting, and sometimes dissolving into unexpected glimpses of clarity.

If you sense playfulness here, it is because truth has taught me that wisdom need not be heavy, it can laugh like a child. If you sense stillness, it is because truth also speaks in silence, like the sky that holds both storm and rainbow.

I share these words not to convince you, but to remind you of something already humming in your own heart. You are not just the doer of actions or the bearer of burdens. You are the experiencer and the experience, the dancer and the dance, the ocean and the waves. You are already whole.

So let us walk together. Not toward achievement, not toward a destination, but into what always was, what always is, into the quiet fullness of being.

Introduction

Namaste!

Before we begin, take a gentle breath. Inhale... pause... exhale... Let the shoulders soften, let the mind settle. You don't need to go anywhere; you've already arrived.

Now, picture this: life is a grand theater, a cosmic carnival. The universe itself is the stage, the spotlight, the script, the actor, and even the audience applauding at the end. You are sitting in the theater seat, watching the drama unfold, and at the same time, you are the play itself. You are the dreamer resting on the pillow of eternity, and also the dream that dances in the night sky.

This is what the ancient sages whispered in forests and what mystics laughed about under starry skies: the essential knowledge. The secret is simple, yet it changes everything. There is no separation. Existence is playing as you, through you, and around you.

When this truth is seen directly, the restless wandering of the seeker ends. It is like tasting water straight from a mountain spring - pure, quenching, leaving nothing more to seek. You don't need libraries of scriptures or lifetimes of effort; one clear sip is enough.

But, if a little voice inside you says, "Wait... this sounds beautiful, but how does it really touch me? How do I live this truth?" then this book is your gentle companion.

It is not meant for the sage who has already dissolved into silence, but for the friend who still feels a longing, a thirst, a playful curiosity to peek behind the curtain. Perhaps you are here because suffering has weighed heavy and you wish to be free. Or perhaps confusion has clouded the mind, and you long for clarity. Or maybe, just maybe, you're here because truth itself called to you like a melody drifting in from another room.

Even if you are not searching for liberation, but simply love the taste of philosophy, the sparkle of paradox, or the sweet dance between science and spirituality, this journey has space for you.

We will walk together lightly. This is not a pilgrimage of effort or struggle. There are no heavy doctrines to memorize or rigid beliefs to cling to. Instead, imagine a lotus slowly opening, petal by petal, in the morning sun. That's how these teachings unfold. With ease. With grace. With playfulness.

First, we will begin with the simple truths, the kind that touch the heart instantly. Then, like divers slipping into a silent blue ocean, we will move deeper into the nature of existence. Not with strain, but with wonder. Not with seriousness, but with the laughter of discovery.

So, take another breath. Let a smile rise, even a small one. The play has already begun, and you are both the star and the audience.

Welcome to this adventure into yourself!

Chapter 1

The Four Paths to Truth

Truth is a mountain.
One peak, many trails.
Each traveler walks by the light of their own nature,
Yet all footsteps are drawn to the same summit.

Truth is one, but paths are many. Just as rivers flow from different mountains yet all merge into the same ocean, so too, humanity has walked different paths to the same reality. The sages saw that no single doorway could serve all. Some are moved by love, some by action, some by silence and some by inquiry. Thus, four great paths were spoken of: each complete in itself yet harmonizing with the others.

The Path of Knowledge (Jnana Yoga)

A sharp flame, cutting through shadow.
It asks: Who am I?
Not body, not mind, not fleeting thought,
but the silent witness, eternal and free.
Here, truth is not gathered,

but uncovered,
like gold beneath the soil.

- Essence: Inquiry into the nature of Self.
- Method: Discrimination between the real and unreal; asking Who am I? Peeling away illusions.
- Practice: Self-inquiry, reflection, meditation on the witness consciousness.
- Outcome: Direct recognition that "I am pure awareness, beyond body, mind, and ego."

On this path, the seeker does not accumulate truths but strips away falsehoods until only truth remains. Like cleaning dust from a mirror, the clarity was always there, only hidden.

The Path of Devotion (Bhakti Yoga)

A river of love flowing toward the Beloved.
It does not question, it sings.
It bows, it surrenders,
it sees the Divine in every face,
in every stone,
in every heartbeat.
Here, the seeker dissolves into song,
and the "I" melts into "Thou."

- Essence: Love of the Divine.
- Method: Surrendering the ego through prayer, chanting, worship, and seeing God in all.

- Practice: Singing hymns, repeating the divine name, offering every action to the Beloved.
- Outcome: Freedom through love, ego dissolves into devotion, and the heart discovers oneness with the Beloved.

For the bhakta (devotee), truth is not dry logic but overflowing love. The final union is not intellectual recognition but the ecstasy of "I and the Beloved are not two."

The Path of Action (Karma Yoga)

The offering of hands, the worship of work.
Every deed becomes prayer,
every gesture an offering.
Not for reward, not for recognition,
but because love acts through you.
Here, ego trims with each selfless act,
and the heart grows light,
unburdened, free.

- Essence: Selfless service.
- Method: Performing one's duties without attachment to results.
- Practice: Daily work offered as service to the Divine or to humanity, without clinging to reward or fear of loss.
- Outcome: Freedom from ego and purification of the heart.

Karma Yoga transforms ordinary life into sacred practice. The act itself is not denied, what changes is the inner stance. "I do, but I am not the doer." Work becomes worship, and service becomes liberation.

The Path of Meditation (Raja Yoga)

The royal road inward.
Step by step,
discipline gathers, breath slows,
the mind becomes still as a moonlit lake.
In that stillness,
the infinite is reflected,
not far, not apart,
but always here.

- Essence: Mastery of the mind.
- Method: Ethical living, discipline, meditation, and concentration (as in Patanjali's Eightfold Path).
- Practice: Breath control, meditation, withdrawal of the senses, stillness.
- Outcome: Union through silence. The restless mind is stilled, and the seeker discovers the luminous presence within.

This is often called the "royal path" because it leads directly into inner stillness. Here, the mind ceases its chatter, and in the silence, the Self shines by itself.

A Comparative Glimpse

- Knowledge (Jnana): Inquiry into Self Discrimination, self-inquiry, reflection. Realization: "I am pure awareness"
- Devotion (Bhakti): Love of the Divine Prayer, chanting, surrender Union through love, dissolution of ego
- Action (Karma): Selfless service Acting without attachment to results Purification, freedom from ego
- Meditation (Raja): Mastery of mind Meditation, discipline, stillness Union through silence, direct experience of Self

In Simple Words

- On the Path of Devotion, you dissolve into love.
- On the Path of Action, you dissolve into service.
- On the Path of Meditation, you dissolve into silence.
- On the Path of Knowledge, you dissolve into truth.

All four are beautiful. But for those drawn to inquiry, to the fire of seeing clearly, the Path of Knowledge is the doorway to direct realization.

What You Gain on the Path of Knowledge

While all paths ultimately meet in the same truth, the Path of Knowledge has its own unique fragrance. It is direct, sharp, and uncompromising.

- Clarity of Vision: You see reality as it is. Illusions fall away. The false identification with body, mind, and story dissolves.
- Freedom from Ignorance: Ignorance (avidya) is the root of suffering. By recognizing yourself as awareness, you are free from fear, grief, and limitation.
- Direct Realization of the Self: The seeker realizes: I am not this fleeting body or restless mind. I am the witness in which all arises and dissolves.
- Inner Peace: When the small self-fades, struggle ends. There is a quiet joy, a natural stillness, independent of outer conditions.
- Liberation (Moksha)

The highest fruit. No rebirth, no bondage, no ignorance. Just the vast freedom of being what you have always been.

Why Walk the Path of Knowledge?

There comes a moment in every seeker's life when the promises of the world, success, possessions, recognition, begin to reveal their limits. They shine brightly, but never for long. Behind each fulfillment, another hunger waits. The heart whispers a question that cannot be silenced: Is there more?

The Path of Knowledge begins exactly here, not with answers, but with the courage to truly ask. This path does not demand belief, ritual, or blind devotion. It invites only a willingness to look, to inquire, to notice what is already present.

Why choose this path? Because it turns the seeker back upon themselves, revealing the silent witness of all experience. While the world offers fleeting pleasures, this path points to what never comes and never goes, the awareness in which all things appear. It is not about adding layers of learning, but about uncovering what has always been here, unnoticed.

The outcome is not some faraway treasure, but a simple, luminous recognition: I am not separate from life. I am life itself. When this realization dawns, the restless search softens. Fear begins to dissolve. Freedom not dependent on circumstances blossoms quietly, like fragrance from a flower.

The fruits of this path are clarity, simplicity, and a joy unburdened by grasping. The mind becomes a servant rather than a master, and the heart learns to dance without condition. To walk this path is to discover that the one who was seeking has always been the one sought.

And so, the Path of Knowledge is not merely a teaching, it is a homecoming. A return to what you already are: awareness, unbroken, infinite, free

On the path of devotion, the heart melts.
On the path of action, the ego fades.
On the path of meditation, the mind stills.
But on the path of knowledge,
the veil itself burns away.
Here you discover:
You are not walking toward truth,
you are truth, walking within itself.
The fruit of this path is freedom,
not found, but revealed.
A freedom so quiet, so complete,

that nothing more is needed.

Many rivers reach the same sea, but this book will travel one stream, the Path of Knowledge (Jñāna Yoga).

Why?

Because it does not ask you to believe, to bow, or to build; it simply asks you to look. This path promises not the accumulation of new truths but the direct recognition of what has always been here.

Step by step, we will not add weight to the mind, but uncover the light that ignorance has hidden.

Chapter 2

The Path of Knowledge

The first step is not a step at all, it's noticing where you already stand.

...Without awareness,
No dawn breaks open the sky.
The sun may rise,
but its warmth never reaches the heart.
Without awareness,
No laughter rings true,
no tears find their holy release.
Awareness,
the silent stage,
the vast emptiness
where life itself performs:
the dance of birth and death,
the music of joy and sorrow.
Awareness,
the unseen witness,
the eternal space
in which all comes and goes,
yet remains untouched...

Take a moment. Close your eyes if you like. Feel the quiet rhythm of your breath. Notice the sounds around you, the hum of life, the gentle weight of your body resting where it is. Thoughts may come and go, feelings may rise and fall, but all of it, every sound, sensation, and thought, is existence showing itself to you.

Existence is vast. It holds mountains and rivers, stars and galaxies, music and silence, joy and sorrow, beginnings and endings. And yes, it also holds you, the one listening, reading, noticing right now. If we wanted to use a single word for this boundless reality, it could be experience because existence always arrives as an experience.

But here is the subtle point: if there is an experience, there must be an experienced. Who or what is it that hears these words, feels the heartbeat, sees the sunrise, dreams the dream?

The ancient sages pointed us toward this mystery: the Experiencer. That quiet, luminous presence within which all experiences arise and dissolve.

It is not a little person inside your head observing like a guard behind a screen. The Experiencer is not separate from life. It is life. Consciousness is not something you "have," like an object you carry. It is the very medium through which everything is known.

Think of it like this: experience and experiencer are two sides of the same coin. The world has meaning only because it is experienced. And the experiencer knows itself only through the richness of experience. You cannot pull them apart, just as you cannot separate the sun from its light.

So, when you ask, "Who is witnessing?" the answer is both simple and mysterious: it is not your body, not your thoughts, not even your familiar sense of "me." It is the open awareness in which all those appear, awareness itself.

This awareness is so close, so intimate, that we often miss it. We chase experiences, pleasures, achievements, memories while overlooking the one constant presence that makes any experience possible. Without awareness, nothing exists for us. No joy, no sorrow, no sense of time. Awareness is the silent stage upon which the entire play of life unfolds.

And here is the beauty: when it is seen that the experiencer is not separate from the world, but is woven into the very fabric of existence, something shifts. The small sense of being an isolated "me" struggling against a vast universe begins to soften. You realize, I am not outside this. I am not other than this. I am both the witness and the witnessed. I am life itself.

This recognition is the doorway to the Path of Knowledge.

It is not about collecting spiritual trivia or memorizing scriptures. It is not about adding more ideas to the mind. It is the opposite, peeling away what is false, what is borrowed, what is unnecessary. Like wiping the dust from a mirror, the clarity is not created, it is revealed.

True knowledge is not something new you acquire. It is the direct recognition of what has always been here: that awareness and existence are one. The experiencer and the experience are not two.

And this path is not heavy, it is playful, luminous. Like a child discovering for the first time that the wave is not separate from the ocean.

So let us walk this path gently, not with strain but with wonder. Not with ambition, but with curiosity and joy. Slowly, step by step, we will discover that peeling away ignorance leads not to complexity, but to simplicity, to clarity, to freedom.

Practice: Watching the Watcher

1. Sit quietly for a minute.
2. Close your eyes and notice a thought arises.
3. Instead of following it, ask: "Who is noticing this thought?"
4. Rest in that silent noticing.
5. Repeat with sensations, sounds, or emotions. This is a glimpse of the Experiencer.

Chapter 3

Qualities of the Seeker

You're not the dancer, you're the dance floor.

Close your eyes for a breath.
Imagine yourself as a garden.

In one corner, the flame of longing glows -
small, steady, unshaken by the wind.
In another, curiosity peeks up
like a fresh green shoot after the rain.

Some flowers are already in bloom -
courage, sincerity, peace.
Others are still curled tight,
waiting for their own season to open.

There is no rush here.
The garden does not compare one flower to another.
It simply grows,
nourished by light,
watered by your sincerity,
and watched over by the sky of awareness...

The path of truth is not just about collecting ideas or repeating wise sayings. Anyone can memorize scriptures, but real wisdom must touch the heart and change how we live. That kind of transformation doesn't happen automatically.

Just like a seed doesn't become a tree without soil, water, and sunlight, a seeker also needs certain qualities to grow. These are not rigid rules. They are like tools, companions, or flowers that slowly bloom as you walk the path.

Let us walk through them one by one, in simple words, with stories you can carry in your heart.

A Burning Thirst for Truth

Every journey begins with longing. Not longing for money, power, or applause, those come and go. The seeker's longing is deeper, like an ache in the heart that keeps whispering:

"Who am I, really? What is this life? What is real?"

This longing is not casual curiosity; it is as urgent as thirst in the desert. Imagine walking for hours under a blazing sun. Your lips are cracked and throat is dry. At that moment, water is not a luxury, it is life itself. In the same way, for the seeker, truth becomes the one thing that cannot be ignored. Everything else fades in comparison.

Buddha's story is a perfect example. He had everything, palaces, music, dancers, gardens filled with beauty. But none of it satisfied him. In the quiet of his heart, he felt empty. That emptiness became a flame. It grew so strong that he left behind his wealth, his titles, his comforts, and even his family, not because he did not love them, but because his thirst for truth was greater than his desire to remain comfortable.

This thirst is the spark that lights the seeker's path. Without it, the journey feels heavy, like dragging your feet through mud. Teachings seem abstract, practices feel dry, and obstacles feel unbearable. But when the thirst is alive, every struggle becomes meaningful. Each difficulty becomes another step toward home, another test of devotion.

This fire gives life to every step. It transforms the seeker's journey from dull effort into a living adventure. With thirst, the seeker is alive, eyes bright, heart awake, spirit unshaken.

A Desire for Freedom

Ignorance is not always obvious. It does not appear as a monster with chains in its hands. It works quietly, like invisible ropes tying us to fear, pain, and false ideas. Because these chains are unseen, most people live with them without even realizing they are bound.

Think of a bird born in a cage. For that bird, the cage is the entire universe. It does not know the vastness of the sky. Only when the bird notices the bars, only when its wings brush against the limits, does the longing to fly awaken.

In the same way, most of us live without noticing how limited we are by our own conditioning. We are ruled by fear: "What will people think of me?" We are trapped by suffering: "I cannot be happy unless life goes exactly as I want." We are blinded by false beliefs: "If I achieve this one thing, then I will be complete." These thoughts become the walls of our cage.

The moment we begin to feel the weight of those chains, the longing for freedom arises. This longing is natural, like a prisoner who, after years in darkness, suddenly sees a sliver of sunlight through a crack in the wall. In that moment, escape is no longer remains a plan, it becomes a necessity.

But this desire is not about running away from life or shirking responsibilities. True freedom is not escape. It is awakening. Just as a sick person long for health, or a drowning man long for air, the seeker longs for a freedom beyond fear, beyond illusion, beyond suffering.

This longing becomes the engine of transformation. Without it, there is no movement.

Curiosity

Curiosity is the freshness of a child's eyes. Watch a child for even a few minutes, they touch everything, ask endless questions, and are never satisfied with one answer. "Why is the sky blue? Why do birds fly? Where does the sun go at night?" Their questions may seem small, but behind them is a deep hunger to know.

This same spirit lives in the seeker. The seeker does not settle for second-hand truths. When someone says, "God is this," or "The world is that" the seeker does not just nod. They ask: "But is it really so? What do I see when I look directly?"

There's a story: A teacher told a child, "The stars are holes in the sky where light comes through." The child smiled politely but then asked, "But who poked the holes?" That's the heart of curiosity, never satisfied with easy or incomplete answers.

Without curiosity, the seeker becomes rigid, locked inside the thought "I already know." That is the end of growth. Life becomes dull, the mind becomes closed.

But with curiosity, even the most ordinary things can open doors to truth. A flower in the garden becomes a wonder: "How does it bloom? What life-force makes it open to the sun?" A passing thought becomes a mystery: "Where did this thought come from? Who is aware of it?" Even a simple stone can become a key to discovery.

Curiosity keeps the seeker fresh, alive, and humble. It is the reminder that life is infinite and every moment can reveal something new if you remain open to look.

Discernment and Clarity

On the path, the seeker must learn to see clearly what is true and what is illusion. Without this clarity, it is easy to mistake shadows for reality and end up walking in circles.

In India, there is a famous example. Imagine walking at night and suddenly seeing a snake lying on the path. Your heart races, your body tenses with fear. But then someone brings a lantern, and you realize, it was only a rope. The snake never existed, yet the fear was real because you believed the illusion.

This is what happens in life. We suffer not only from reality itself, but often from the stories we project onto it. We mistake appearances for truth. We imagine threats where there are none, or cling to beliefs that have no foundation.

Discernment is like the lamp. It doesn't fight with the darkness, it simply shines. When light is present, illusions dissolve on their own.

In daily life, discernment shows up in small ways. For example:

- Someone criticizes you. Without clarity, you immediately feel hurt and angry. With clarity, you pause and ask: "Is their criticism true, or is it just their opinion?" Already, the sting is less.
- You read or hear spiritual claims. Without discernment, you may believe blindly. With discernment, you test them in your own experience before accepting.

Discernment also protects the seeker from two traps: blind superstition and blind skepticism. Both are extremes. One believes without question; the other dismisses everything without question. Clarity is the middle way, it neither clings nor rejects blindly, but looks, tests, and sees.

A seeker without discernment is like a traveler without a compass, they may walk a lot, but they won't know if they're headed in the right direction. With discernment, every step is sure, because it rests on seeing things as they are.

An Open Mind

A closed mind is like a window that has been shut for years, the air inside grows stale, the room becomes dark, and nothing fresh can enter. An open mind is like opening that window and letting in the breeze of truth. It brings light, freshness, and the possibility of seeing life in a new way.

There is a famous Zen story. A university professor once visited a master to learn about Zen. The professor began talking about all the books he had read, all the philosophies he knew. The master quietly poured him a cup of tea. He kept pouring until the tea overflowed, spilling onto the table.

"Stop!" the professor cried. "The cup is full, no more can go in!"

The master smiled and said, "So is your mind. How can I show you truth unless you first empty it?"

This is the heart of openness. If you already think you know, learning is impossible. But when you set aside pride and certainty, space opens for new understanding.

Openness doesn't mean swallowing everything without thought. It doesn't mean being gullible. Instead, it means listening deeply, welcoming possibilities, and then using discernment to test what feels true.

For example:

- If someone shares a perspective different from yours, a closed mind rejects it immediately: "That can't be right." But an open mind says: "Let me listen. Maybe there's something here I haven't seen before."
- If life brings an unexpected challenge, a closed mind says: "This is only a problem." An open mind asks: "Could this also be a lesson? What can I learn from it?"

An open mind is not weakness, it is strength. It is the courage to admit, "I don't know everything. I am willing to see." In truth, the open mind is the doorway to wisdom. Only when the window is open can the light come in.

Self-Inquiry

A true seeker does not only question the world outside, but they also turn inward and ask: “What am I holding on to that may not be true? What fears shape the way I live? What stories do I keep telling myself that may be illusions?”

This is the essence of self-inquiry: shining the light of awareness on your own mind.

Think of a room that hasn’t been cleaned in years. The furniture may be beautiful, the windows wide, the carpets rich but everything is covered in layers of dust. Until the dust is cleared, the beauty of the room cannot be seen. In the same way, the mind is full of dust, old fears, second-hand beliefs, childhood conditioning, and unexamined assumptions. Unless you clean it, wisdom remains hidden under layers.

Self-inquiry is the broom and the duster. It clears space so that truth can shine. It can be very simple.

For example:

- You may notice, “I always avoid speaking up in meetings.” Instead of blaming circumstances, self-inquiry asks: “What fear is behind this? Am I afraid of judgment? Do I believe my voice doesn’t matter?”
- Or you may find yourself chasing endless achievements. Self-inquiry pauses and asks: “What am I really running after? Do I believe that success will finally make me complete?”

Every time you ask sincerely, illusions lose their grip.

There is a Zen story: A student asked his master, "What is the path to truth?" The master replied, "Who is asking?" That one question turned the student's attention inward, where the real search begins.

Self-inquiry is not about judging yourself harshly. It is about seeing clearly. It is gentle but fearless looking. And the more you look, the more you discover that behind the layers of dust, your essence has always been pure, open, and free.

Intelligence and Common Sense

Wisdom is like a bird. It needs two wings to fly. One wing is intelligence, the ability to see far, to understand deeply, to ask big questions about life and existence. The other wing is common sense, the ability to live wisely in everyday situations—handling relationships, money, work, and ordinary challenges with balance. Without both wings, the bird cannot fly.

Many people lean too much on one side. Some are very intelligent, but without common sense they become impractical. They may talk brilliantly about philosophy, or describe the stars and galaxies, but if they cannot show kindness to their neighbor, keep their promises, or manage the simple needs of life, their wisdom feels incomplete.

On the other hand, some people are very practical but lack the curiosity or openness to see beyond daily survival. They may manage life's details well, but they miss the deeper questions: "Who am I? What is the meaning of all this?" Without intelligence, life remains flat and limited.

Real wisdom is the harmony of both. It is the ability to wonder about infinity and remember to wash your cup after tea. It is being able to think about the nature of the soul and know when to comfort a friend who is hurting. It is reading sacred texts and also knowing how to live with honesty and kindness in small, daily acts.

Great teachers of the past were never only dreamers; they were also deeply practical. They could speak of the highest truth, but also show you how to walk, eat, and live-in harmony. True wisdom shines in the way you treat people, in the way you handle small things, in the way you live your ordinary life.

Sincerity and Determination

The path of truth is not smooth. It has deserts of doubt, storms of fear, and mountains of difficulty. Sometimes the way ahead feels endless, and it is tempting to turn back. Many seekers begin with enthusiasm but stop halfway when challenges arise.

What helps you keep going are two companions: sincerity and determination.

Sincerity is the compass. It is the inner honesty that keeps you pointed toward truth, even when distractions try to pull you away. A sincere seeker does not walk the path to impress others, gain status, or collect spiritual titles. Their heart is simple: "I want to know. I want to see." That purity is what gives direction, like a compass needle always pointing north.

Determination is the strength of the journey. It is the power to keep moving, step by step, even when the road is rough. Think of a river. When it meets a rock, it does not stop and complain.

It flows around it, over it, or through it, always finding a way forward. That is determination: steady, patient and unstoppable.

History is full of examples. Buddha spent years wandering, fasting, and searching. Many times, he could have turned back, but sincerity kept his vision clear, and determination gave him the endurance to sit under the Bodhi tree until truth revealed itself.

Even in ordinary life, you see this pattern. A student who sincerely wants to learn will keep studying despite failures. An athlete who longs to succeed trains even when tired. A mother who loves her child finds strength to keep going, no matter how difficult the circumstances.

In the same way, the seeker who walks with sincerity and determination may stumble, may get tired, may even fall. But they never give up. And in time, sincerity becomes light in the darkness, and determination becomes the steady strength that carries them across deserts and mountains to the home of truth.

Discipline and Self-Mastery

Discipline is often misunderstood. People think of it as strict rules, rigid control, or punishment. But in truth, discipline is freedom.

Imagine water. When it spills everywhere, it cannot move a wheel or turn into power. But when it flows in a riverbed, focused and steady, it has strength. In the same way, without discipline our energy leaks into a hundred distractions, endless scrolling on social media, gossip, chasing desires that never satisfy. With discipline, that same energy gathers, flows, and carries us toward truth.

Discipline is not about saying "no" to life. It is about saying a clear "yes" to what matters most. It is choosing direction over distraction, depth over surface.

Self-mastery is the natural fruit of discipline. But it does not mean repression or denying your humanity. A person who represses desires only pushes them deeper, where they become stronger. Self-mastery is different. It is a balance. It is the ability to enjoy without being enslaved, to act without being driven by impulse, to rest without falling into laziness.

Think of a skilled musician. At first, they practice scales daily with discipline. The repetition feels hard. But slowly, their fingers learn, their ear sharpens, and one day they can play freely, beautifully. The discipline has become self-mastery and now it has turned into harmony.

The seeker too begins with effort: waking up early for meditation, learning to pause before reacting, resisting the pull of distractions. At first, it feels like effort. But over time, it becomes natural, like a river flowing easily to the sea.

In daily life, self-mastery shows itself in small ways:

- Eating with awareness instead of out of habit.
- Choosing silence when anger rises.
- Knowing when to let go of a thought or desire that no longer serves.

Discipline is the path; self-mastery is the flowering. Together, they bring freedom.

Courage

To walk the path of truth, a seeker needs courage. Not the loud, showy courage of battlefields, but the quiet, steady courage of the heart.

Seeking truth often means questioning what everyone around you takes for granted. It means daring to ask: “Is this belief really true? Is this custom truly necessary? Is this the whole of life, or is there more?” That questioning can be uncomfortable. Families may resist, friends may laugh, society may judge. To keep walking despite that pressure takes courage.

History gives us shining examples. Socrates, the great Greek philosopher, was condemned to death for encouraging people to question blindly accepted ideas. Offered a chance to escape, he refused. He calmly drank the poison, choosing truth over survival. His life still whispers to us: better to die in truth than to live in illusion.

But courage is not the absence of fear. A person without fear is not brave, they are simply unaware. Real courage is different. It is feeling fear fully yet moving forward anyway. Fear whispers in your ear, “Stop, it’s too risky, you’ll fail, you’ll be rejected.” Courage answers quietly, “Yes, I hear you, but I will take the step.”

Even in daily life, courage shows itself in simple ways:

- Speaking honestly when silence feels safer.

- Admitting "I don't know" instead of pretending.
- Standing alone when the crowd goes the other way.
- Facing your own inner shadows rather than running from them.

A seeker without courage remains stuck in comfort zones. A seeker with courage grows wings. For it is courage that carries you across the thresholds of fear into the open space of truth.

Reverence for Knowledge and Teachers

Knowledge is not just information, it is sacred. For the seeker, wisdom is like water in the desert: precious, life-giving, and never to be taken for granted. A true seeker approaches knowledge with respect, whether it comes from a living teacher, a book, a line of poetry, silence, or even from nature itself. Sometimes a single bird in flight, a flower opening, or a child's laughter can carry a teaching deeper than a thousand words.

There is an old saying: "When the seeker is ready, the guru appears." This doesn't always mean a person in robes or with titles. Teachers can appear in unexpected forms, a friend's advice at the right time, a stranger's kindness, or even a painful failure that teaches you what nothing else could. Life itself becomes the teacher. Reverence does not mean blind obedience. Blind following leads to dependence, not freedom. Instead, reverence means listening with humility, honoring the gift of learning, and receiving wisdom with gratitude. Gratitude is what transforms knowledge from dry words into living truth.

Think of it like this: if you drink water carelessly, spilling most of it, you remain thirsty. But if you drink with care and gratitude, every drop nourishes you. In the same way, when knowledge is received with reverence, it becomes nourishment for the soul, not just ideas for the mind.

Great teachers of the past always taught respect for the teaching itself. Not worship of the personality, but reverence for the truth being shared. A humble "thank you" to the wisdom received keeps the heart open, and in that openness, deeper truths can enter.

For the seeker, reverence turns learning into a blessing. It changes every lesson, whether joyful or painful, into a step on the path of awakening.

Simplicity and Focus

A cluttered life leaves little room for wisdom. When our days are filled with endless noise, possessions, and unnecessary busyness, the heart has no space to rest. Simplicity is not about living with nothing, it is about living with clarity, choosing what truly matters and letting go of what doesn't.

A pond cannot reflect the moon if its waters are disturbed by constant ripples. Only when it is still does the moon shine clearly upon its surface. In the same way, when life is simplified, when unnecessary noise is quieted, the heart becomes calm enough to reflect truth.

Simplicity does not mean denying life's beauty. It doesn't mean you cannot enjoy comfort, food, music, or companionship. It means you are no longer buried under things you don't need, distractions that don't serve, and thoughts that only create confusion.

Focus is the companion of simplicity. Once the clutter is cleared, your attention is free. Instead of scattering energy in ten directions, you give yourself fully to what matters whether it is listening deeply, meditating, or simply drinking a cup of tea with awareness.

The wise have always lived simply, not as a rule but as a natural choice. When your heart is uncluttered, joy comes more easily, peace feels natural, and truth reveals itself without struggle.

Attention and Expression

A seeker must first learn to listen. Not just to the words people speak, but also to the silences in between. Not just to books and teachings, but to life itself, to the rustle of leaves in the wind, to the rhythm of the breath, to the quiet pulse of the heart.

Attention is presence. It is like holding a lamp steady. If your handshakes, the flame flickers and shadows dance on the wall. You cannot see clearly. But when the lamp is steady, everything is revealed just as it is. In the same way, when your attention is steady, truth shines through the simplest moments.

Most people miss life not because it is hidden, but because they are not paying attention. A flower blooms, but the eyes are glued to a screen. A friend speaks from the heart, but the mind is already elsewhere. Truth slips fast and unnoticed.

For the seeker, attention is like a sacred key. It turns ordinary moments into windows of insight. Drinking a cup of tea becomes meditation when you are fully present. Walking becomes prayer when you notice each step, each breath.

Expression is the natural partner of attention. When the seeker speaks, it is not to impress or to display knowledge. Their words carry the weight of sincerity. They speak simply, like someone offering water to the thirsty.

There is a story of a Zen master who gave long, complicated lectures. Few understood him. One day, a student asked another master, "Why don't you speak with such brilliance?" The master smiled and replied, "Because truth is simple. Why cover it in decorations?"

When words arise from attention, they have clarity. They do not confuse, they reveal. They do not inflate the ego; they serve the listener. In this way, attention and expression together make the seeker's life both a lamp and a gift.

Peacefulness and Non-Violence

A restless or aggressive mind is like a stormy lake. Waves rise, winds howl, and the water is full of turbulence. In such a lake, the reflection of the sky is broken and unclear. Only when the water is still can the sky be mirrored perfectly. In the same way, only a peaceful mind can reflect truth clearly.

Peace is not weakness. It is inner strength, the kind that cannot be shaken easily. When the mind is restless, even small problems feel overwhelming. But when the mind is peaceful, even great challenges can be faced with clarity and balance.

Non-violence is the natural expression of peace. Many think it only means "not hurting others," but it goes deeper. It also means not being violent toward yourself. How often do we scold ourselves harshly, judge ourselves unfairly, or push our bodies beyond their limits? A seeker learns gentleness, not just outwardly, but inwardly too.

To live in non-violence means:

- Speaking words that heal instead of harm.
- Acting with kindness instead of aggression.
- Treating your own heart with compassion instead of constant criticism.

A seeker who cultivates peace becomes like a calm garden where wisdom can take root. And from that soil of peace, compassion and understanding naturally grow.

Care for the Body

The body is the temple of awareness. Without it, you cannot taste food, hear music, breathe deeply, or sit in silence. It is the vessel through which life is experienced. That is why the seeker learns to treat the body not as an enemy to be fought or as a toy to be indulged, but as a sacred companion on the journey.

If neglected, the body becomes a burden. Illness, fatigue, and imbalance make it hard for the mind to stay clear. Imagine trying to light a lamp in a broken stand; the flame will flicker and sometimes goes out. In the same way, awareness cannot shine steadily if the body is weak or ignored.

Caring for the body does not mean obsession with fitness or beauty. It means balance and respect. The seeker nourishes the body with healthy food instead of overindulgence, rests when tired instead of pushing endlessly, and moves with exercise to keep energy flowing. It is a simple rhythm: eat with awareness, sleep with gratitude and walk with presence.

There is a saying from the Zen tradition: "When hungry, eat. When tired, sleep." It sounds simple, but in truth, most people eat without awareness and push themselves to exhaustion. The seeker learns to honor the body's natural wisdom.

Think of the body as a loyal horse carrying you through the journey. If you mistreat it, whip it, or ignore its needs, it will collapse on the road. But if you feed it well, care for it, and let it rest, it will carry you far and steady.

The body is not the goal, but it is the foundation. With respect and balance, the body supports awareness like a strong lamp holding a steady flame.

Stability in the World

A seeker is not only spirit. They live in the world too. To walk the inner path while ignoring the outer is like trying to build a temple in the sand. It cannot stand for long.

Stability is the foundation. It is like the roots of a tree. A tree may grow tall, spreading its branches toward the sky, but if the roots are shallow, the first storm will topple it. Only when the roots are strong can the branches rise fearlessly.

For the seeker, these roots are threefold:

- Financial independence: Not endless wealth, but enough to live with dignity, without constant anxiety over survival. A seeker who is burdened with money worries cannot easily sit in peace.

- Emotional maturity: The ability to meet life's ups and downs without being carried away by every wave. A stable heart becomes a safe ground on which wisdom can grow.
- Ethical integrity: Living in truth, keeping promises, acting with honesty. Without integrity, the seeker is divided within themselves, and divided soil cannot nurture growth.

Imagine someone who wants to meditate but is constantly worried about paying bills, or someone who speaks of truth but deceives in business. How can their inner search go deep? Just as a bird cannot fly well with a broken wing, a seeker cannot

soar in truth without worldly stability.

This doesn't mean chasing wealth, perfection, or status. It means living responsibly, with balance, so that the practical parts of life support the spiritual journey instead of pulling it down.

With strong roots, the seeker can rise high stretching toward the sky of truth without fear of falling.

Moral Values

Truth cannot blossom in the soil of dishonesty. Just as a seed cannot grow in polluted ground, wisdom cannot take root in a life built on lies, arrogance, or cruelty.

Moral values are not a list of imposed rules. They are the natural fragrance of a sincere heart. Kindness, humility, honesty and compassion are not the burdens. They are companions that walk with the seeker, guiding them gently along the path.

Without values, knowledge becomes sharp but hollow. It is like a sword, powerful, but dangerous if used without care. A clever person may win arguments, but without kindness their words become weapons. On the other hand, knowledge rooted in values is like food nourishes, strengthens, and sustains life.

Consider this: two people may study the same scripture. One uses it to dominate and control others; the other uses it to bring comfort and healing. The words are the same, but the heart behind them makes all the difference.

There is a story told of a saint who was asked, "What is the proof that someone has found truth?" He replied, "Watch how they treat others. If wisdom makes them more kind, more humble, more honest, then it is real. If it makes them proud or harsh, it is only borrowed knowledge, not living truth."

Moral values are the ground on which all other qualities grow. They steady the seeker, protect against self-deception, and ensure that wisdom becomes a blessing to all, not just a possession of the self.

When kindness, humility, and honesty flow naturally, the seeker's life itself becomes teaching silence, fragrance, and true.

Conclusion: The Inner Garden

A seeker is not a checklist of qualifications. No one begins the path with everything "in order." A seeker is more like a fragrance. Something subtle, alive, and unique.

These qualities that we have spoken of, thirst, curiosity, openness, courage, peace, and many others are like flowers in an inner garden. Some bloom quickly, like wildflowers after the first rain. Others take time, like trees that grow slowly but stand for centuries. And that is perfectly natural.

You don't need to perfect these qualities before walking the path. In fact, the path itself is what ripens them. Walking on this path waters the flowers. With each step, with each honest effort, with each mistake and each realization, the garden inside begins to blossom.

Think of the lotus. It does not open all its petals at once. It unfolds slowly, petal by petal, in its own rhythm, in its own time. In the same way, the being of the seeker opens naturally, through patience, sincerity, and love.

There is no rush. There is no competition. A true garden grows quietly, steadily, and beautifully. So does the seeker.

Practice: Lighting the Inner Flame

1. Place your hand gently on your heart.
2. Ask yourself: "What do I truly want to know?"
3. Notice if a longing, a question, or a quiet pull arises.
4. Breathe into that flame.
5. Let it remind you that sincerity is more important than perfection.

Chapter 4

The Ideal Seeker

The Bow of Humility

Sit for a moment, still.
Feel the weight of your body,
the rhythm of your breath.
Inside you, imagine a gentle bow,
not bending in shame,
but in openness.
A bow that whispers:
"I am ready. I do not know. Teach me, Life."
With this bow,
the whole world becomes a teacher.
The bird's song becomes scripture.
The passing cloud becomes
a lesson in impermanence.
A mistake becomes a mirror.
Even silence begins to speak.
The ideal seeker is not the one with answers,
but the one who never stops listening.
Every breath is a verse.
Every step, a chance to awaken.

The journey of knowledge is never a one-way street. A guru does not simply pour wisdom into a seeker's head like water into an empty cup. True learning is alive. It is relational. It is fluid. It is a dance.

The teacher can point the way, inspire, question, and challenge. But the seeker must also move, must take the steps, must join the dance. Without participation, wisdom remains only words on a page, never becoming lived truth.

It is not about being the most "intelligent" person in the room. In fact, intelligence without humility often becomes arrogance, a closed door that no wisdom can enter. What teachers truly look for is something subtler, more fragrant, more human: a living attitude. A fire in the heart. A sincerity that says, "I am willing to learn, to be changed, to let go of what I thought I knew."

The ideal seeker is not the one who knows the most, but the one who is most willing to not know. To stay open. To be vulnerable. To be curious. For an empty space is what allows fresh water to be poured in.

There is a Zen story of a master who told his students, "Do not come to me with your hands full. Come with empty hands. Only then can I give you something new." The same is true of the mind. When it is cluttered with certainties, there is no space for wisdom. But when it is open and willing, transformation becomes possible.

So let us look at the qualities of such a seeker, not as rules to follow, but as seeds. Every seeker already carries these seeds within. With the right soil of sincerity, the sunlight of openness, and the water of practice, they begin to sprout, grow, and blossom into the fragrance of true learning.

The Dedicated and Eager Seeker

Teachers are not drawn to cleverness, to quick answers, or to sharp arguments. What draws them is sincerity, the quiet, steady glow of a heart that longs for truth.

A dedicated seeker is one who returns again and again. Not for praise. Not for recognition. Not even to impress the teacher. They return because something inside will not let them rest until they touch what is real. Their dedication is not forced; it is a natural pull, like a river flowing toward the sea.

Dedication has its own fragrance. It creates a field of receptivity, a kind of readiness. Imagine soil that is rich, moist, and alive and when a seed is planted there, it does not struggle to grow. It takes root, sprouts, and blossoms naturally. In the same way, when knowledge falls into the heart of a dedicated seeker, it takes life at once.

Such a seeker does not treat wisdom as private property, to be hoarded or guarded jealously. Instead, they become a bridge. They carry the flame forward, not by clinging to it, but by lighting other flames. Their dedication ensures that knowledge does not stop with them, it continues, spreading warmth and light through time.

A dedicated seeker becomes like a lamp in the dark. They absorb light with humility, and in turn, they shine, not for themselves, but for all who walk near them.

Inherent vs. Developable Qualities

Some qualities are already woven into us before our first cry as a newborn. They arrive with us, quiet but alive like seeds resting deep in the soil of the heart, waiting for the rains of awareness to awaken them. These are inherent qualities.

Others are not present from the start but can be grown. They are developable qualities planted with intention, nurtured with care, strengthened through time and practice.

The inherent ones are like a secret fragrance, always present even if unnoticed. A deep hunger for truth that no comfort or achievement can fully satisfy. An inner yearning to break free from the invisible chains of ignorance and suffering. A subtle, guiding whisper, soft as a breeze that nudges us toward light when we wander too close to shadow. These are not learned; they are remembered, as if they were always part of us.

The developable ones are like tender branches reaching for the sun. They grow with attention and practice. Curiosity that keeps the eyes fresh with wonder. Clarity and logic, like a polished mirror, reflecting truth and exposing illusion. Patience to endure when the path feels long. Focus to stay steady amid distractions. Discipline to return again and again when the mind strays. Resilience to rise after each fall. These qualities are built slowly, like muscles strengthened through steady exercise.

The beautiful secret is this: even the faintest spark within us is never lost. It may lie hidden for years under the ashes of distraction or doubt, but it remains. All it needs is a gentle breath to awaken it into flame.

A teacher is not someone who gives you truth. No one can hand that over, because it is already yours. A teacher is more like a catalyst, someone who helps you see what was always present within you. Think of it like a fire hidden under ashes. The teacher does not create the fire; it is already there. What the teacher does is blow gently, remove a little of the covering, and remind you to look again. Suddenly, the flame that

seemed lost comes alive, and you realize it was never absent.

The real role of a teacher is not to add something new, but to help you recognize what you already carry. The path has always been inside you. The teacher simply helps you notice it.

The Snowball Effect of Knowledge

In the beginning, the path of learning can feel like an uphill climb. Each step is met with resistance. The mind argues, the body hesitates, and the heart questions: Is it worth the effort? Doubts whisper softly, yet persistently: Perhaps this is too difficult. Perhaps I am not ready. Distractions appear like glittering stones on the roadside, luring attention away from the mountain's ascent.

And yet, something within insists on moving forward. The first taste of knowledge, however small, shifts the balance. Like a seed discovering rain, the soil of awareness begins to soften. One drop of wisdom makes the next easier to receive. The mind that once resisted begins to open; the heart that once questioned begins to lean forward.

Knowledge has its own gravity. It draws you toward itself, gently but irresistibly. Each insight prepares the ground for a deeper one. Clarity begets clarity, and slowly, the scattered fragments of understanding begin to join, forming a whole. What once felt like a slow climb begins to reveal its hidden momentum.

Imagine a snowball at the top of a mountain. At first, it is small, fragile, uncertain. It requires effort to shape, and care to set in motion. But once released, it gathers speed. With every turn, it collects more snow. Its weight increases, its momentum expands, and soon what was once a fragile ball becomes an unstoppable force rolling freely down the mountain.

So too with knowledge. At first, the effort is conscious, deliberate. You must hold yourself to discipline, return again and again when the mind drifts. But then something miraculous happens, the learning begins to carry itself. The more you know, the more you want to know. The more you see, the more your eyes open. Curiosity, once faint, becomes alive and insistent.

This is the snowball effect of knowledge: a movement from effort into flow, from resistance into eagerness. The joy of discovery becomes its own nourishment. Learning ceases to be a task and becomes a celebration. No longer do you climb the mountain, you find the mountain itself carrying you, as if life conspires to roll you into greater and greater depths of understanding.

The seeker discovers that wisdom is not a finite treasure to be acquired, but a living fire that grows brighter the more it is fed. And with each spark, curiosity awakens further, transforming the journey itself into joy.

The Trap of Ignorance

Ignorance is not simply the absence of knowledge; it is a refusal to see. It is like closing the eyes in full daylight and saying, "There is no sun." It is not darkness itself, but the stubborn choice to remain in darkness even when light is available.

It clings to comfort: "Better the prison I know than the freedom I do not." It fears being wrong: "If I question, I may have to change." It resists the unknown, because the unknown feels vast, uncertain, threatening to the fragile structures of certainty the mind has built.

Imagine a man sitting in a cave, surrounded by shadows. He has lived there so long that the flickering shapes on the walls are his world. To him, they are reality. When someone whispers, "There is more. There is a sky beyond these walls," he laughs in disbelief. The cave is safe, predictable. The sky is terrifying because it is unknown. And so, he chooses the familiar darkness over the risk of light.

This is the essence of ignorance.

- Those without curiosity will not ask, and so the cave walls remain unchallenged.
- Those without openness will not listen, and so the whispers of truth pass them by.
- Those without discipline will circle endlessly, tracing the same patterns on the floor of the cave, mistaking motion for progress.

Ignorance feeds on inertia. Like water left standing in a pond, it grows stagnant. Like a wheel turning without direction, it spins but goes nowhere. It prefers sleep to wakefulness, illusion to reality, repetition to transformation.

And yet, the trap is more fragile than it appears. One spark can break it. One question born of curiosity, one act of courage, one breath of sincerity can pierce the shadows. Like a candle lit in a dark cave, even the smallest flame reveals the walls, the exit, the vastness beyond.

Ignorance cannot survive the presence of light, because darkness has no substance of its own. It is only the absence of seeing. The moment a seeker dares to open their eyes, even a little, the illusion begins to crumble. The cave is seen for what it is: a shelter, perhaps once useful, but no longer a home.

And beyond the cave, the sky awaits. Limitless, open and infinite.

Stepping into the Light

When even a single spark arises, the cave no longer feels the same. What once seemed safe begins to feel small. The shadows that once entertained now appear empty, repetitive, unreal. Curiosity awakens like a breeze in still air, whispering: “What lies beyond?”

The first step is always the hardest. It means leaving behind the comfort of what is known, even if what is known is suffering. The familiar has its own gravity; it pulls you back again and again. Yet the heart longs for something greater, something truer. And when that longing grows stronger than fear, the journey begins.

To step into the light is not to acquire new knowledge, but to release old illusions. It is not adding more but letting go of what never was. As the eyes adjust, the brilliance of reality can feel overwhelming. There may be pain in seeing how long you remained in shadow. But slowly, what was blinding becomes natural, what was hidden becomes clear.

You discover that ignorance was never a wall. It was only a veil, woven of habit and fear. Pull one thread, and the veil unravels. The light has always been there, waiting.

And in the vastness of sky, something shifts. You realize you are no longer just a seeker looking for lessons, you are life itself learning to recognize its own nature. The teacher is everywhere: in the bird crossing the horizon, in the breath rising in your chest, in the silence between thoughts.

The cave was never the end of the story. It was only the beginning, the place where you gathered the courage to awaken.

Cultivation as Transformation

To cultivate these qualities is not to chase perfection. The path is not about becoming a "perfect seeker," but about becoming a living learner. Perfection is rigid, like a statue, silent, unmoving. But learning is alive, flexible, and ever-growing. The true seeker is not carved in stone but shaped like a tree, rooted, yet always reaching and always unfolding.

Discipline sharpens clarity, like a blade honed against the whetstone of practice. Without it, the mind grows dull, scattered, lost in distraction. Discipline is not harshness, but steadiness, the willingness to return, again and again, to what matters.

Curiosity keeps the heart fresh, like spring water bubbling endlessly from the earth. It prevents wisdom from becoming stale, keeps learning alive and playful. Without curiosity, knowledge turns into dry repetition. With curiosity, every moment becomes new, every encounter a doorway.

Courage makes the path possible. It is the fire that allows the seeker to step beyond the familiar and face the unknown. Without courage, we cling to comfort, to what we already know, circling endlessly in the same patterns. With courage, the horizon opens, and the heart dares to walk into light.

Humility ensures that wisdom does not become ego's newest disguise. Without humility, even knowledge can harden into pride, turning truth into a weapon rather than a mirror. But with humility, wisdom remains fragrant, gentle, receptive and able to serve.

In this process, teachers are not the only guides. Life itself becomes the Guru. Every joy, every failure, every heartbreak, every delay is a teaching. Success reveals one kind of truth, failure another. Obstacles polish the soul. Sorrow deepens compassion. Time itself chisels away, what is false, shaping and refining until the seeker is no longer separate from the path.

In the end, cultivation is not about achievement. It is transformation. Slowly, silently, steadily, the seeker dissolves into the learning, until there is no longer a seeker and the sought, no longer two, but one unfolding stream of awareness.

Conclusion: Becoming the Path

The ideal seeker is not an exam-taker, measuring life in scores and achievements. The ideal seeker is a truth-lover, whose very being leans toward what is real. Qualities may be given as seeds at birth, or they may be cultivated through effort and practice, but together they prepare the ground not for borrowed knowledge, but for lived insight.

To be a seeker is not to collect wisdom like coins in a jar, but to allow wisdom to reshape you completely, silently, from within. At first, you carry teachings in your mind and memory. Later, you begin to live them in your words and actions. And finally, the boundary dissolves. You no longer carry wisdom; you are wisdom. The river no longer flows past you. You have become the river itself.

Step by step, the seeker disappears into the path. The seeker and the sought merge. There is no longer an "I" chasing truth and a "truth" to be found. There is only the unfolding of awareness, walking within itself, learning from itself, rejoicing in itself.

This is the promise of the path: when you cultivate these qualities, discipline, curiosity, courage, humility, you are not simply preparing to learn. You are preparing to awaken. And in awakening, you discover that there was never really a journey at all. Only life itself remembering what it always was.

To be a true seeker is to allow wisdom to transform you. Slowly, step by step, you move from carrying wisdom... to being wisdom.

This is the promise of the path: in cultivating these qualities, you are not just preparing to learn, you are preparing to awaken.

Practice: Beginner's Eyes

1. Pick a very ordinary object nearby (a cup, a pen, your hand).
2. Look at it as if you've never seen it before.
3. Notice colors, shapes, textures without naming them.
4. Imagine you are a seeker seeing the world anew.
5. This cultivates openness, curiosity, and humility—the eyes of an ideal seeker.

Chapter 5

The Loom of Knowledge

From Survival's Knowledge to the Horizon of Mystery
Sit quietly.

Imagine your mind as a library, rows and rows of books.
Each book is a memory, a lesson, a piece of knowledge.
Now imagine a window in that library.
Outside, a vast sky, endless and unknowable.
The books are precious,
but the sky is infinite.
Breathe deeply.
Bow to both:
the books that guide you,
and the sky that forever humbles you.

Having looked at the qualities of the seeker and the understanding of an ideal seeker, let us now turn to knowledge itself. What is this strange flame we seek? How does it form, grow, and guide? To walk the path of wisdom, one must first understand the very nature of knowledge, its strengths and its pitfalls

The Evolutionary Gift

In the beginning, knowledge was simple, immediate, and practical. For our earliest ancestors, it was the thin line between life and death. To remember that fire burns was to protect the hand. To know that the snake bites was to guard the foot. To recognize that one plant heals and other kills was to preserve the body and pass life forward. These were small packets of organized experience like primitive threads woven just tightly enough to form a fabric of survival. Knowledge, in its earliest form, was earthy, urgent, rooted in necessity. And yet, something miraculous stirred within the human mind. The same capacity that held memory for survival began to ask questions that stretched beyond survival. We lifted our gaze from the ground to the sky and wondered:

Why is the sky so vast?
What lies beyond the stars?
Who am I, behind this body and breath?

Knowledge, once only a shield, became a flame. It carried us beyond the hunger for food to the hunger for truth, beyond the need for safety to the longing for meaning. What began as protection for the body blossomed into liberation for the soul.

Knowledge and Its Formation

But what is knowledge, truly? Knowledge is not passive. The mind does not sit as a still mirror, reflecting reality exactly as it is. Rather, it is a loom, ceaselessly weaving. Every impression that enters, every sound, every sight, every touch, is compared, connected, given meaning.

A sound is tied to a name.
A touch is bound to pain or pleasure.
A cause is linked to its effect.

Each thread is small, fragile, almost invisible. But together, the threads form a fabric. This fabric is what we lean upon when we say, "I know." It is not a single impression that grants knowledge, but the pattern that arises when impressions are joined. And this fabric is never finished. Each new experience rearranges it, thickens it, sometimes tears it apart. At times it must be rewoven when false threads create distortion. To "know" is not to possess a fixed certainty, but to live in the continual weaving of meaning.

Knowledge is alive, breathing, always in motion. Too rigid, and it hardens into dogma. Too loose, and it unravels into confusion. Its strength lies in its living adaptability, firm enough to guide action, open enough to be rewoven when truth demands.

How Knowledge Organizes Itself

This weaving does not happen randomly. Our mind organizes experiences in patterns, turning the chaos of impressions into a web of order. Through these patterns, meaning is born:

- **Name ↔ Object** – A word maps to a thing. "That is a book."
- **Action ↔ Actor** – Agency is seen. "The dog chased the cat."
- **Cause ↔ Effect** – "Touch fire → pain." The foundation of survival and science alike.

- **Subject ↔ Object** – "I read the book." The eternal dance of observer and observed.
- **Classification** – Cats, dogs, birds. Rice, wheat, barley. Simplifying the vast into kinds.
- **Abstraction** – "Justice," "gravity," "love." Concepts beyond touch or sight, yet real in their shaping of life.
- **Discrimination** – Choosing what nourishes, avoiding what harms; in food, in thought, in relationship.
- **Hierarchy** – From family trees to cosmic orders, structuring reality into layers and ladders of meaning.

These eight threads form the great web of knowledge. The tighter and more interconnected the web, the clearer our movements become. The weaker and more fragmented it is, the more we stumble. Knowledge is not merely stored, it is woven, arranged, structured into coherence.

The mind is the loom, continuously weaving, and what emerges is the living cloth of understanding upon which we walk through life.

The Fragile Balance

Yet this fabric is delicate. Knowledge must also carry stability, or else it collapses into illusion. If what we call knowledge shifts like sand, it cannot be trusted. To "know" today that the sun rises in the east and tomorrow to insist it rises in the west is not knowledge but confusion.

True knowledge carries a kind of stillness. It is steady, like a mountain. It can adapt, like a tree bending in the wind, but it does not uproot itself with every passing breeze. It can expand, refine, and even transform with new discovery, but under scrutiny it does not collapse.

The seeker must therefore guard against mistaking opinion for knowledge, belief for truth, or assumption for reality. These are fragile imitations, easily broken. Knowledge must be tested, lived, confirmed, and integrated. Only then does it shine with coherence. Only then does it become the lamp that does not flicker in every wind.

The Cumulative Gift

Knowledge is not only stability, it is growth. It is cumulative, a layered inheritance. A child learns language word by word. Words gather into sentences. Sentences give rise to thought. Thought gives birth to meaning. Each layer rests upon the last, creating a scaffold for the next.

This layering allows us to move beyond what our senses can touch. A child learns fire burns by feeling its heat. But through accumulated knowledge, humanity can now imagine stars burning billions of miles away. I may never place my hand upon a black hole, yet through the cumulative gift of knowledge, I can sense its pull, imagine its hunger, and glimpse its reality.

Each generation inherits more than life. It inherits the scaffolding of all who have come before. We walk across bridges built by countless seekers, standing on stones laid long before our time. Knowledge does not imprison us in the past; it propels us forward into the unseen.

This is the great gift: knowledge stretches us beyond immediacy, beyond survival, beyond the limits of our own brief lives. It opens realms we will never touch yet can still know.

The Three Realms of Knowing

All that exists can be placed into three great baskets. Together, they hold the whole mystery of life.

The first is the Known. This is what we have already touched, tasted, and lived. It is the world familiar to us, the warmth of fire on the skin, the taste of salt on the tongue, the sound of rain on the roof, the memory of yesterday's joys and sorrows. The known is our foundation, the ground on which we walk with confidence. It is the steady thread of experience that gives us stability, identity, and belonging. Without the known, life would be chaos. But if we cling only to the known, we soon grow rigid, repeating the same patterns without wonder.

The second is the Unknown. This is what lies ahead, waiting to be discovered. A new species hidden in the forest. A star not yet mapped by the astronomers. An insight that suddenly blooms in the heart after years of seeking. The unknown is not emptiness. It is a possibility, an open horizon stretching endlessly before us. For the seeker, the unknown is the call to adventure, the invitation to grow. Each step into it expands the boundaries of life. Without the unknown, life would be stale. But if we fear the unknown, we shrink into the prison of the familiar.

The third is the Unknowable. This is what forever escapes the grasp of thought, not because it is distant, but because it cannot be measured. It is the silence before the first word was spoken, the mystery behind all appearances, the infinite that no concept can contain. The unknowable humbles us. We often avoid it, for it reminds us of our limits. Yet to bow before the unknowable is itself a form of wisdom. It teaches reverence, reminding us that no matter how much we know, or how much remains unknown, there is always that which cannot be grasped.

When the seeker stands before the unknowable, there is no arrogance, no possession. Only awe. And in that awe, wisdom flowers. The wise do not shrink from the unknowable; they kneel before it. For in its presence, the mind softens, and the heart opens to mystery.

Positive and Negative Knowledge

Knowledge wears two robes, one of light, one of shadow. Both are needed on the path of clarity.

Positive Knowledge affirms. It says: "This is so. The sun shines. Fire gives warmth. Water quenches thirst. The sky is blue." It adds to our understanding, building the structures of learning piece by piece. This is the kind of knowledge we collect in schools, in books, in daily life, knowing how to cook a meal, how to drive a car, how to read the stars.

Negative Knowledge denies. It says: "This is not so. The sun does not shine at night. The earth is not flat. A shadow is not a ghost but the absence of light." It strips away illusions, clears false paths, and removes errors that block the way forward.

Curiously, negative knowledge is often the more reliable guide. What we affirm as true today may be corrected tomorrow. For centuries it was "known" that the earth was flat, or that the sun moved around us. Positive knowledge evolves and sometimes shifts with new discoveries.

But when a falsehood is exposed, it rarely returns. Once we know the earth is not flat, the illusion is gone. Once we see a shadow for what it is, fear disappears. Negative knowledge is like pulling weeds from a garden. Once cleared, the soil is ready for truth to grow.

Everyday life offers countless examples:

- Science advances not only by affirming new truths, but by disproving old errors. Newton's physics gave way to Einstein's, yet the falsehood that the earth is flat will never return.
- In relationships, clarity often comes by seeing what is not love like control, fear, or dependence. Removing these illusions makes space for genuine love to appear.
- On the inner path, self-inquiry often begins not with affirmations, but with negations: "I am not this body. I am not this thought. I am not this fear." Each "not this" removes a false layer, until what remains is the simple presence of awareness itself.

Like a sculptor carving marble, truth is revealed not by adding but by subtracting. The statue was always within the stone. The sculptor only removed what did not belong.

Thus, both robes of knowledge are needed:

- The affirming hand that builds, step by step.
- The denying hand that clears, strike by strike.

Reflection: Beyond Knowledge

Knowledge has been humanity's great gift. In the beginning, it was about survival. But over time, it grew into something larger: a way of making sense of life, asking deeper questions, and reaching beyond survival toward meaning.

Knowledge is alive. Like a river, it flows and reshapes the land. Like a loom, it weaves patterns out of experience. If too rigid, it hardens into dogma. If too loose, it unravels into confusion. But when tended well, it brings clarity, steadiness, and direction.

And yet, knowledge is not the final destination, it is a bridge. It builds structure and prepares the ground, but its true purpose is to lead us toward wisdom. Just as scaffolding falls away once a temple is built, knowledge too must eventually give way.

Wisdom begins where knowledge dissolves into lived experience. Reading about love is not the same as loving. Studying maps of the ocean is not the same as diving into its depths. Knowledge points the way, but wisdom is the walking, the living, the being.

For the seeker, this is the threshold: the moment of turning from gathering to embodying, from concepts to silence, from ideas to direct seeing. Knowledge must be cherished, but not clung to. Its highest gift is not to remain in the mind, but to open the heart to truth.

And so, the journey continues. Knowledge has carried us far, but now it invites us to step beyond where wisdom shines, not as something learned, but as the very light of awareness itself.

Practice: Knowing and Not Knowing

1. Bring an apple (or any simple object) in front of you.
2. First, recall everything you "know" about it: name, taste, color, science, history.
3. Then, hold it silently. Feel its weight. Smell it. See it freshly.
4. Finally, whisper: "What do I not know about this apple?"
5. Let the mystery be as alive as the knowledge.

Chapter 6

Means of Knowledge

Discerning True Gateways from Illusions on the Path of Knowing

Close your eyes.

Imagine walking down a hallway lined with doors.
Some are painted in beautiful colors, carvings, shining handles.
You push them, but they do not open. They are illusions.
Others look plain, even dull. Yet when you turn the handle, the door swings open to vast light.
Ask yourself gently:
Which doors in my life are painted illusions?
Which ones, simple and steady, open into truth?
Breathe. Smile. Trust the plain, the simple, the true.

Knowledge is not only what we gather, but how we gather it. The means matter. A thousand impressions may pass through the mind in a single day like conversations, news, teachings, memories, but only some ripen into truth. The rest remain clutter, fragments of information that cloud more than they clarify.

Think of a diamond picked up in the dark. To the hand, it feels like any other stone. Only when light shines upon it does its brilliance become clear. In the same way, the manner in which we approach experience determines whether it becomes wisdom or remains mere memory. The light we bring through attention, purity of perception, and openness of heart, makes truth visible. Without that light, even precious experiences pass by unnoticed.

The sages of old spoke of this as the valid means of knowledge. They knew that not all ways of knowing are equal. Some are true doors, leading into reality. Others are only painted doors bright and attractive, but when you try to enter, they open onto nothing.

The mind is full of such painted doors. Opinion masquerades as certainty. Habit disguises itself as truth. Desire whispers what it wants to hear and calls it knowledge. Without discernment, the seeker wanders in a hall of mirrors, mistaking reflections for reality.

To walk wisely is to learn to tell the difference. A true door may not dazzle the eye, but when you lean on it, it opens. It does not trap the seeker in belief; it reveals what is. Painted doors, though beautiful to look at, collapse when tested.

This is why the path of knowledge is not only about accumulation but also about discernment. Not every stone must be carried. Not every voice must be believed. Not every path is worth treading. The seeker must learn to test the doors of perception, to knock, to wait, to see which opens into light.

For it is not enough to know. One must know rightly. And it is not enough to gather truth. One must gather it in such a way that it ripens into wisdom, shining clear and steady in the heart.

Valid Means of Knowledge

The sages of old taught that it is not enough to collect impressions; one must know how knowledge is born. Just as a seed requires good soil, water, and sunlight to grow, knowledge too requires the right conditions, the right doors through which truth can enter. Here are the two valid means of gaining knowledge:

Direct Experience

There is no substitute for touching reality directly. To see the sunrise, you must open your eyes. To taste a mango, you must bite into it. No poem, no explanation, no memory can replace the living taste of the fruit itself.

Our senses are the first gateways: sight, sound, touch, taste and smell. Through them, reality enters us, fresh and unfiltered. And today, our reach extends further: microscopes open worlds that are too small for the naked eye, telescopes reveal galaxies too vast for human sight, sensors detect vibrations beyond the range of hearing. Even the mind itself becomes an instrument, reflecting truths not always accessible to the senses, as in meditation or intuitive flashes of clarity.

Direct experience is raw. It is the foundation stone upon which all other knowledge rests. Without it, all reasoning, all testimony, all imagination is adrift. The seeker must learn to return again and again to experience itself, to touch the real rather than settle for echoes.

Logic

Experience gives us the raw material; logic shapes it into meaning. Logic is the thread that weaves impressions into patterns, making them coherent and dependable.

It connects the dots:

- Where there is smoke, there must be fire.
- If footsteps echo, someone must have walked here.

Sound reasoning guards us from illusion. It arranges the flow of impressions into structures that hold, testing whether our understanding is stable or collapses under scrutiny.

Yet logic does not create truth, it only reflects and tests it. A flawless argument built on false assumptions can still mislead. But when married to the direct experience, logic becomes the second wing of the bird of knowledge.

Together, direct experience and logic are two wings of the bird. Without either, the bird cannot fly. With both, it soars, rooted in reality, guided by reason, able to cross the sky of understanding with grace and balance.

Invalid Means of Knowledge

Not every doorway that appears before us leads into truth. The seeker must learn to tell the difference, for mistaking false doors for real ones is the root of much confusion.

Imagination

Imagination is a gift, a luminous power of the mind, the birthplace of poetry, music, and visions of possibility. Without imagination, there would be no art, no discovery, no dream of what might be.

But when imagination is mistaken for knowledge, it misleads. Dragons and fairies, cosmic conspiracies and fantasies of power may stir the heart or amuse the mind, but unless they are grounded in direct experience and tested by reason, they remain shadows of fancy.

Imagination is a fire. It can illuminate, or it can burn. Used rightly, it inspires exploration. Used blindly, it fabricates illusions mistaken for truth. The seeker must honor imagination for what it is: a tool of creation, not a proof of reality.

Assumptions and Beliefs

Assumptions are shortcuts the mind takes when it does not want to pause. Beliefs are inherited which are passed down by family, culture, tradition, or authority. They offer comfort, a ready-made map of the world. But when left untested, they become fog upon the path.

The seeker must pause and ask with sincerity:

- Did I experience this directly?
- Is it supported by reason?

If the answer is no, then what we hold is belief, not knowledge. And belief without inquiry hardens into bondage. It closes the eyes instead of opening them, making us cling to maps drawn by others instead of exploring the territory ourselves.

Belief, like imagination, has its place that can inspire devotion, preserve wisdom, and guide conduct. But if mistaken for knowledge, it blinds. For the path of truth demands not inherited answers but living inquiry.

Knowledge grows only when the seeker dares to test, to question, to strip away the painted doors and find the openings that lead to light.

Teachers, Books, and External Sources

A teacher is not a fountain pouring wisdom into a student's vessel. A true teacher is a lamp, pointing you back to your own eyes, your own reasoning, your own direct experience. They illuminate the path, but they cannot walk it for you.

Books and scriptures are like footprints of those who walked before. They can inspire and guide, but they are not final proof. In today's world where information pours endlessly from every screen, discernment is more essential than ever. Not every word carries the fragrance of truth. The seeker must learn to separate inspiration from confirmation, map from territory.

The Purified Mind

Even the best instruments fail if they are clouded. A telescope smudged with dust blurs the stars. A mirror fogged with steam cannot reflect the face clearly. Likewise, a mind clouded by fear, agitation, or prejudice cannot perceive truth as it is.

This is why traditions across the world emphasize śhuddhi - purification. Meditation, self-reflection, discipline, and simplicity are not punishments; they are practical cleansings of the mirror. A calm mind is like still water: it reflects reality exactly as it is.

At the same time, the seeker must strengthen the instrument of reason. Just as muscles grow stronger with use, clarity of thought develops through practice. Questioning deeply, thinking carefully, and resting patiently in inquiry train the mind to stay awake and steady in the presence of truth.

The Power of Questions

Questions are lamps for the seeker. A dull question produces shadows; a sincere one illuminates the way.

The timeless seven questions: What? Why? How? When? Where? Who? How many? are simple, yet profound. With them, ignorance is chipped away piece by piece, like stone from a statue.

But more important than the technique is the courage behind the question. A living mind dares to ask even when the answer might unsettle. To question is to open a door. To refuse is to remain in a locked room. A seeker's vitality is measured not by how much they already know, but by how alive their questions are.

Knowledge of Absence

There is also a subtler way of knowing: the knowledge of what is not.

When you open the fridge and see that the milk is missing, you gain knowledge. Not by presence, but by absence. Absence speaks with its own clarity. It removes errors, corrects assumptions, and directs the seeker to look elsewhere.

This way of knowing is easily overlooked, for the mind is trained to chase presence, what is seen, touched, and affirmed. Yet the silence between sounds gives music its rhythm. The pause between breaths is as vital as the breath itself. The spaces between words allow meaning to be heard.

Absence, too, teaches. It sharpens awareness like a whetstone against the blade. When something expected is not there, the mind awakens from habit and begins to look more carefully. The missing becomes a doorway into deeper seeing.

Thus, silence often speaks louder than speech. Emptiness often carries more weight than form. The seeker learns not only from what appears, but also from what does not appear. To notice absence is to refine perception, to let subtlety become the teacher.

For in the end, absence is not empty, it is full of hidden presence.

Metaphors as Bridges

Metaphors are bridges, not destinations. They help the mind cross from the familiar to the unknown, from what is seen to what is unseen.

To tell a villager, "A city is like a larger village," may help them imagine something beyond their direct experience. Yet no matter how vivid the description, it is not the city itself. To walk its streets, to hear its noise, to taste its food alone reveals the living reality.

So too with truth. Scriptures, poetry, and teachings are filled with metaphors: the Self is like space, the mind like a restless monkey, wisdom like a lamp. These images are not the reality, they are only fingers pointing. The finger may show the way to the moon, but the finger is not the moon.

The danger is in mistaking the bridge for the destination, the metaphor for the truth itself. Then the seeker clings to the symbol and never steps into what it points toward. Words become idols, and the living experience is lost.

The wise remember: metaphors are gifts, but their purpose is to be crossed. Once the other shore is reached, the bridge is no longer needed.

Thus, let metaphors guide, but not bind. Let them awaken longing but not replace seeing. For in the end, truth is not a story, not a symbol, not even a teaching. Truth is the direct encounter, silent, immediate, beyond comparison.

Conclusion: The True Means

The true means of knowledge are simple, yet they hold tremendous power like small keys that open vast gates.

Direct experience is the first. It is raw, immediate, unfiltered contact with reality. To see the sunrise is not the same as reading about it; to taste a mango is not the same as hearing it described. Direct experience is truth knocking at your door without an interpreter. When the eyes are clear, when the senses are awake, reality pours in fresh and alive.

Logic and reflection follow as the guardians of coherence. Experience is rich, but without reflection it remains scattered like pearls on the ground. Logic threads them into a necklace, giving continuity and meaning. Reflection is not cold calculation but a deep, contemplative seeing: Does this truly fit? Does this align with what I already know of life? Logic is the mind's way of bowing to order, of refusing to let confusion masquerade as truth.

Questions are the seeker's lamps. Where certainty blinds, questions illuminate. A simple "Why?" has toppled empires of superstition; a single "How?" has given birth to science. Every great discovery whether of gravity, of love, or of God, began as a question. The mind that does not question is a closed room; the mind that asks is a window flung wide open to the breeze of truth.

And finally, there is the purified mind, the still water that reflects reality without distortion. Imagine a pond on a stormy day; the surface is broken, and even the most beautiful mountain cannot appear clearly. Now imagine the same pond on a quiet morning, still as glass; every detail of the mountain is mirrored perfectly. So, it is with the mind. A restless, fearful, or clouded mind distorts reality. A quiet, centered mind reflects it as it is. Meditation, discipline, and awareness are the polishing cloth that clears this mirror.

Together, these four; experience, reflection, questioning, and purification are not complicated methods, but natural movements of consciousness. They are the seeker's compass and lamp, ensuring that knowledge does not remain borrowed or secondhand, but becomes lived, tested, and true.

False means imagination mistaken for fact, assumptions, blind belief that may decorate the path, but they do not open real doors.

When the seeker learns to discern, to trust direct experience while sharpening reason, knowledge blooms naturally. It is not imposed but revealed.

Science as a Living Example

- **Direct Experience:** Galileo dropping spheres from the Tower of Pisa was direct observation. He didn't just accept Aristotle's belief that "heavier objects fall faster." He tested it.
- **Logic:** Einstein didn't travel at the speed of light, but through reasoning he concluded relativity, then it was confirmed through experiments.
- **Invalid Means:** For centuries, people believed the Earth was the center of the universe because it "looked that way." That was an assumption, not a tested truth. Only when observation and logic aligned did we move past it.

- **Lesson:** Science progresses when curiosity replaces blind acceptance. Beliefs collapse under experiments; truth stands.

Everyday Life Examples

- **Imagination vs Reality:** You hear a noise at night. Imagination says: "There's a ghost!" Direct experience (turning on the light) shows it's just the wind.
- **Assumption vs Test:** You assume "coffee always wakes me up." But if you pay attention, you'll notice sometimes it makes you jittery or anxious. Experience + logic refine the belief.
- **Knowledge of Absence:** You reach for your phone in your pocket and it's not there. That absence is knowledge, as powerful as presence, telling you to look elsewhere.

Lesson: Much of our stress comes from mistaking assumptions or imagination for knowledge. Testing them often reveals surprising clarity.

Modern World Examples

- **Fake News & social media:** Many people share headlines without checking sources. This is belief without inquiry. Valid knowledge asks: "Did I verify? Does it align with fact and reason?"
- **Medicine & Health:** Some trust "miracle cures" because they sound convincing. Real medicine demands evidence:

trials, data, peer review. Without experience and logic, we fall prey to illusion.

- **Technology:** GPS tells you a route. Sometimes, it's wrong. Direct experience (you see a closed road) overrides the "belief in the map." The wise traveler uses both tools together: data plus observation.

Lesson: In an age of overflowing information, discernment is the modern seeker's most precious tool.

Inner Path Examples

- **Meditation:** A teacher may say, "Meditation brings peace." That is belief. But sitting down and experiencing it yourself is direct knowledge.
- **Self-Inquiry:** You may assume, "I am always anxious." But by observing your breath or mind, you may notice moments of calm. Direct seeing corrects the false assumption.
- **Spiritual Metaphors:** Scriptures often speak in metaphors ("the Self is like space"). Beautiful pointers, but only direct experience reveals what they mean.

Lesson: The inner journey is not about collecting second-hand truths but verifying them in lived experience.

Practice: The Door Test

1. Recall a belief you hold strongly. It could be small ("coffee wakes me up") or big ("happiness depends on success").
2. Ask: "Is this from direct experience, or only assumption?"

3. If it is from experience, test it with logic: “Does it always hold true? Under what conditions?”
4. If it is from belief, trace its source: family, culture, imagination?
5. Simply notice which of your “doors” open to truth, and which are only painted illusions.
6. This playful practice trains the seeker to tell the difference between valid and invalid means of knowledge: one of the most essential skills on the path.

Chapter 7

The Illusion of Knowledge

From Endless Noise to Living Knowledge

Between words and silence,
Between maps and the land,
Truth waits, untouched by noise,
A song only lived, never borrowed.

We live in an age of endless streams: books, podcasts, blogs, tweets, reels, and courses on every imaginable subject. The world has never spoken so loudly, so continuously. Every moment, something new arrives to demand our attention.

The irony? Humanity has more information at its fingertips than ever before, yet so often we find ourselves more restless, more anxious, more fragmented. We scroll and scroll, but do not feel nourished. We consume endlessly but remain unsatisfied. The mind becomes a crowded marketplace where voices shout, but no true conversation occurs.

Why? Because information is not knowledge.

Information vs. Knowledge

You can memorize the world's great scriptures yet remain unchanged. You can read a hundred recipes yet never taste the fragrance of cooking. You may collect countless quotes yet still miss the silence from which truth speaks.

Information points. Knowledge is lived.

- Information is a map.
- Knowledge is the journey.
- Wisdom is arriving at the destination and realizing the map itself was only a hint.

The difference is subtle, yet immense. A map is helpful, but it is not the land. You cannot smell the rain-soaked earth of a forest through lines of ink. A recipe is useful, but it is not the taste. A scripture is sacred, but unless its words are lived, it is only ink on paper.

Information comforts the mind by giving it something to hold, but knowledge transforms the being by changing the way you live.

The Limits of Information

Information without context is empty. Words in a language you do not know are only lines of ink. A formula in physics means little until you have felt the wonder it describes. Like a shadow on a wall, information suggests reality but it cannot replace reality itself.

A map of Paris is not Paris. To know Paris, you must walk its streets, sip its coffee, breathe its air, and hear laughter echo through alleys at midnight. Until then, Paris remains an idea, a picture in the mind, not a living truth.

So, it is with life. Information alone leaves us standing outside the door, staring at the key. We may carry the key in our pocket, polish it, describe it in detail but until the door is opened, we remain in the hallway of speculation.

Knowledge begins only when the threshold is crossed, when the room is entered, when life itself is touched.

The Problem with Intellectual Knowledge

Here lies the seeker's greatest temptation: to confuse intellectual mastery with transformation. The mind delights in collecting concepts, arranging them neatly like butterflies pinned in glass cases. Yet the fluttering of wings is lost; the life has been stilled.

Reading a thousand books on meditation is not the same as sitting still for ten minutes. Watching endless videos about love is not the same as holding someone quietly, heart to heart, without words. Listening to discourses on silence is not the same as tasting silence in your own breath.

Concepts are like shadows on the cave wall, suggestive, intriguing, but not the real. Only experience is sunlight. A shadow of fire can never warm your hands; a picture of water can never quench your thirst.

This is why Osho playfully said: "Don't just chew the menu—eat the food." The menu may describe flavor, aroma, nourishment, but only eating brings satisfaction. Intellectual knowledge is the menu; lived experience is the meal.

The Danger of Misinformation

The modern world does not merely overflow with information, it drowns in misinformation. Half-truths, distortions, and confident lies travel faster than facts. What once spread slowly by word of mouth now circles the globe in seconds, wrapped in headlines, dressed in certainty, carried on the wings of algorithms that feed appetite, not accuracy.

A polished speaker can make fiction sound like truth. A viral post can reshape opinion overnight, whether it rests on reality or not. And once planted, a falsehood can linger long after it has been disproven, like an echo that refuses to fade.

For the seeker, this is a subtle and dangerous trap: mistaking illusion for insight, opinion for wisdom, noise for knowledge.

Thus, every piece of information must be tested:

- Does this align with direct experience?
- Does it hold steady in the light of reason?

If it fails these tests, it is not knowledge but noise shimmering on the surface, empty at the core.

The Necessity of First-Hand Experience

No one learns to swim by reading books. You may study the strokes, memorize the theory of buoyancy, even recite the physics of water but until you step into the river, until the current presses against your skin, until your body discovers its own rhythm, swimming remains only an idea.

No one learns balance on a bicycle through lectures. You may watch others glide, hear explanations of momentum, listen to advice on posture but real learning begins only when you wobble, when you fall and scrape your knees, when you rise again and again, until at last balance arrives like a silent gift.

So, it is with all knowledge worth having. It must be lived, not borrowed.

Borrowed knowledge is like borrowed fire, it warms for a moment but soon fades. The flame must be your own, lit in the hearth of your own experience. Otherwise, it dies with the departure of the source.

True knowledge is always first-hand. Scriptures, teachers, books, and guides may point, but until you live it, the truth remains someone else's.

The Trap of Information Overload

Today, many seekers have become collectors. They gather teachings like shells on a beach, book to book, video to video, teacher to teacher. Each new fragment of wisdom excites the mind, but few take root in the heart.

They forget: no tree grows by collecting seeds alone. Seeds must be planted, watered, and lived. A pocket full of seeds is potential, not nourishment.

A cluttered mind stuffed with untested teachings is like a kitchen counter covered with ingredients that never touch the flame. Ingredients without fire do not make a meal. So too, teachings without practice never become wisdom.

Information may fill the shelves of memory, but wisdom is born only when digestion occurs, when truth is absorbed and integrated into the very blood of life. Wisdom is digestion, not collection.

The Need for Skepticism and Inquiry

For a seeker, the real strength does not lie in collecting words or bowing to authority, but in questioning with a living, alert mind. Knowledge is not something to be swallowed whole; it must be tasted, tested, and proven in the fire of experience. Without this, it is easy to be swept away by persuasive voices, attractive appearances, or half-truths that glitter but do not nourish. Information is like a faint echo. Skepticism checks whether the echo has substance. Curiosity invites us closer. And only when we live it does it become real knowledge.

True skepticism is not negativity; it is compassion for truth. It clears away illusion so that reality can be seen without distortion. The sincere seeker is not hungry for endless piles of words but for vision that eyes see clearly, without fog.

Closing Reflection: From Data to Living Truth

The illusion of information is seductive. It makes us feel full while leaving us empty. True knowledge is quieter, subtler, and far more demanding. It asks not for storage, but for transformation.

To unveil true knowledge is to let go of the glittering surface and dive into lived depth. To read less and see more. To collect less and live more. For the real journey of knowing is not about what passes through the mind, but about what awakens in the heart.

Information is a river flowing endlessly, but the seeker does not drink all water blindly. They pause, cup their hands, taste, and see. True knowledge blossoms when information touches life. It becomes not something you "have," but something you are. And when knowledge ripens fully, it flowers into wisdom, a living intimacy with existence itself.

Information is a shadow. Knowledge is the light. Wisdom is the sun itself.

Practice: From Menu to Meal

1. Recall one piece of information you encountered recently, a teaching, a fact, a quote.
2. Ask: "Have I lived this, or do I only know about it?"
3. If it is only borrowed, find one way to test it in real life today. Apply it, even in a small way.
4. At day's end, reflect: "What changed when I lived this?"
5. This is how information transforms — from borrowed words into living truth, from menu into nourishment, from shadow into light.

Chapter 8

The Fluid Nature of Truth

Living in the World While Resting in the Witness

Truth is a mirror,
shifting with the gaze.
Sometimes River, sometimes sea,
yet always water,
always whole.

We speak of truth often, but rarely pause to ask: What do we really mean by it? Is truth a fact, a feeling, a law, or a revelation? Is it the same for the scientist as for the poet, for the child as for the sage?

In daily life, we divide the world quickly into "true" and "false." If something fits our expectations, confirms our habits, or behaves in ways we can predict, we label it true. If it unsettles us, challenges our assumptions, or breaks the familiar pattern, we dismiss it as false.

Yet in doing so, are we discovering truth or only defending our comfort? Who, then, decides what is true? And by what measure?

Is it the mind, with its logic?
The heart, with its sincerity?
The senses, with their testimony?

Or is truth something deeper still, something that outlives every perspective?

Perhaps truth is not an object waiting to be found, but a living mirror reflecting differently depending on how and where we look.

How We Choose What's "True"

Truth is not a single stone lying in the universe, fixed and waiting to be picked up. It is shaped by the eyes that look, the mind that measures, and the heart that feels.

For a scientist, truth is weighed by data, measured through instruments, tested in repeatable experiments. What holds again and again under scrutiny is honored as truth.

For a lawyer, truth emerges from evidence and testimony, the weaving together of stories until a pattern of credibility appears.

For a lover, truth is not in data or testimony, but in the raw honesty of a touch, a glance, a heartbeat.

For a child, truth is whatever sparks wonder, bubbles rising in the air, rain tapping the window, the magic of the first snowfall.

The same event can appear as true for one person and false for another. Not because reality itself has changed, but because the lens through which it is seen is different.

That is why the sages have said: truth is alive, not rigid. Like water

Relative and Absolute Truth

The sages of many traditions spoke of truth in two dimensions: the shifting and the eternal, the practical and the profound.

Relative Truth (Vyāvahārika Satya)

These are the truths of daily life, the agreements and conventions that allow human beings to share a common world. Without them, communication would collapse and society would dissolve into chaos.

- "The train leaves at 7."
- "This medicine reduces fever."
- "Water boils at 100°C."

Such truths are practical, contextual, and often provisional. They help us coordinate action, exchange meaning, and navigate the circumstances of living. Relative truth belongs to the realm of language, measurement, and agreement.

It is the truth of commerce and calendars, of science and medicine, of law and custom. It tells us how to grow crops, how to build bridges, how to treat illness, how to conduct rituals, how to greet one another. These truths are indispensable in daily life, they create the fabric of order, cooperation, and predictability.

And yet, relative truth is never absolute. It shifts with time, culture, and perspective. What is true in one age may be false in another:

- Once it was “true” that the Earth was the center of the universe.
- Once it was “true” that disease was caused by evil spirits.
- Even today, what is considered polite in one culture may be offensive in another.

Relative truth is therefore functional, not final. It is like a compass: useful for pointing direction, but not the journey itself. A compass can show “north,” but it cannot walk the mountain path for you, nor can it reveal the taste of the spring at the summit.

For the seeker, the great danger is mistaking relative truth for ultimate truth. Maps are mistaken for the land, words for reality, doctrines for the ineffable. But just as a finger pointing to the moon is not the moon itself, so too relative truth must always be seen as a guide, not the destination.

To honor relative truth is wisdom, for without it we cannot live together. But to confuse it with the absolute is bondage. The art of the seeker lies in using relative truths skillfully, while never forgetting their provisional nature.

Relative truth helps us live in the world. Absolute truth (Pāramārthika Satya) shows us what the world itself arises from.

Absolute Truth (Pāramārthika Satya)

Beyond these shifting agreements lies something that does not move. Absolute truth is the ground beneath all appearances, the witness that remains when forms come and go. Beyond shifting agreements and provisional maps lies something that does not move. Absolute truth is not bound by culture, language, or time. It is not a product of thought, nor dependent on measurement or consensus. It is the ground beneath all appearances, the silent witness that remains as forms arise and dissolve.

- "I am."
- "Awareness is the constant witness."
- "That which changes cannot be ultimate."

These are not statements of belief, but direct recognitions. They point to what is immediate, unshakable, undeniable. Long before we say "I am this" or "I am that," there is simply "I am." This self-evident fact of being is absolute truth: prior to name, prior to form, prior to identity.

Relative truths are like signposts along a road. They guide, they indicate, they help the traveler. But the absolute truth is the ground upon which the road itself is built, the earth that supports all paths yet belongs to none.

Teachers often begin with relative truths, for the mind needs stepping stones. They point, they compare, they explain. Yet their final gift is not another concept, but the unveiling of what has always been here, the luminous simplicity of the absolute.

Relative truth shifts with context, like the reflection of the moon in moving water. Absolute truth is the moon itself, untouched, steady, and whole.

Inferior and Superior Criteria for Truth

Not all measures of truth are equally trustworthy. Some are fragile, built on hearsay or habit; others are strong, grounded in lived seeing.

Inferior criteria are the most common because they are the easiest:

- Believing in something simply because it is written in a book.
- Accepting it because the authority has declared it.
- Trusting it because many repeat it.

These forms of "truth" may provide comfort, but they rest on shaky ground. Rumors can spread faster than facts, dogma can survive for centuries without proof, cultural conditioning can shape entire lives without ever being questioned. Such truths are like houses built on sand; they may appear stable until the first strong wind arrives.

Superior criteria demand more of us, but they give much more in return:

- **Direct experience**: What is seen, felt, and lived cannot be dismissed so easily. To see the sunrise is different from reading about it.

- **Reason and logic**: Coherence across time and space; truth that holds together rather than collapsing under contradiction.
- **Consistency and repeatability**: A truth that can be tested again and again, like fire that always burns or water that always quenches thirst.

The seeker's task is to move from the inferior to the superior, from borrowed truth to the tested truth, from secondhand beliefs to firsthand seeing.

It is like moving from sketches to the living landscape itself. Words and beliefs may point, but only direct vision confirms. To rely on inferior criteria is to live in shadows; to embrace the superior is to walk in the light of what is.

The path of inquiry is nothing more and nothing less than this movement: a steady turning away from the borrowed toward the lived, from comfort toward clarity, from illusion toward reality.

The Simplicity of Truth

Relative truths are often tangled in detail. They need careful explanations, long justifications, endless exceptions. "This is true only in this circumstance, only at this temperature, only under these conditions..." Relative truths shift like patterns in sand, beautiful but easily disturbed.

Absolute truth, on the other hand, is breathtakingly simple. Such truths do not depend on conditions, arguments, or proof. They shine by their own light.

And yet, this very simplicity often feels unbearable to the restless mind. The mind is addicted to complexity. It seeks doctrines, philosophies, systems, layers upon layers of explanation. But absolute truth is like a clear sky, so vast and open that the mind, used to clouds, does not know how to rest in it.

A teacher's role, then, is often not to add more but to subtract. To peel away layer after layer of complication until the seeker stands naked before what has always been here.

Truth itself does not need adornment. It is the mind that craves decoration. The work of the path is simply to recognize the brilliance of what is already shining, too simple to be believed, too obvious to be noticed.

The Freedom of Certainty

When we lean on sound criteria, direct experience, reason and consistency, life gains a quiet steadiness. The ground beneath our feet feels firm. Decisions lose their heaviness, for they arise from clarity rather than confusion. Actions flow with more confidence, as if guided by an unseen rhythm.

But when the absolute is glimpsed, when awareness recognizes itself, something deeper happens. The entire game of truth and falsehood is seen in a new light. Life becomes play. Nothing needs defending, nothing needs proving. There is no longer the urgency to convince, to argue, to guard. Truth does not fight for itself; it simply shines. The sun does not argue with shadows, it only waits for clouds to pass.

Dancing with Two Truths

Truth is not a rock, hard and immovable, but a river, ever-flowing, ever-shifting. At one level, it bends and adapts to the contours of life, winding through the valleys of circumstance. At another, it is the vast ocean that holds all rivers, the stillness that never moves.

- Relative truth is the compass we use to navigate the practicalities of living.
- Absolute truth is the silence in which all compasses dissolve.

Both are needed. Both are sacred. Relative truth gives us language, agreements, and shared worlds. Absolute truth reveals what we are when all words fall away.

The wise one does not cling to either extreme. They move fluidly between them, using relative truth with compassion yet resting inwardly in absolute truth with peace. Like a dancer who knows the stage is made of wood but moves as if it were infinite sky, the awakened one lives in both realms at once.

Meditation: Resting in Two Truths

Sit quietly for a few moments. Feel the body as it is, its weight on the chair, the rise and fall of the breath. This is **relative truth**: the body, the sensations, the flow of thoughts and emotions. They are here now, shifting moment by moment.

Now, turn attention to the one who notices. Who is aware of this body, this breath, this passing thought? Notice that awareness itself does not come and go. Thoughts move, the body changes, sensations arise and pass but awareness remains. This is absolute truth: the unchanging witness in which all change appears.

Hold both together gently, without conflict:

- The relative: this breath, this room, this moment of life.
- The absolute: the silent awareness that holds them all.

Rest in this dance. Relative truth lets you live; absolute truth lets you be free. Both are real, both are necessary, both are part of the play.

When you open your eyes, carry this remembrance: you are both the river that flows and the ocean that holds it.

Practice: Testing Truth

1. Think of something you consider "true." It could be small ("coffee wakes me up") or large ("success brings happiness").
2. Ask: "By what criteria am I calling this true? habit, culture, logic, or experience?
3. Test it: Does it hold in all situations, or only some? Is it relative or absolute?
4. Finally, sit silently and ask: "What is true that never changes, no matter what?"
5. Notice how truth can be relative for daily life, yet behind it all, something silent and absolute shines.

Chapter 9

The Unchanging Amidst Change

Seeing Beyond the Dance of Forms

Forms flicker,
memories fade,
but essence waits,
silent, unshaken,
the ground beneath the dance.
There is a principle so simple,
it almost feels too sharp.

"What changes is not true."

At first glance, it sounds severe, almost unreasonable, to call the changing unreal. After all, everything around us moves and transforms. Seasons turn from spring to summer to autumn to winter. Rivers carve new paths with every flood.

People are born, grow, love, wither, and pass away. Even within us, cells die and renew themselves each moment. Change is not the exception; it is the very pulse of life.

So why did the sages declare that all that changes is false?

Not because change is meaningless, nor because the world is to be dismissed. But because truth, if it is ultimate, cannot be temporary. That which fades was never absolute, it belonged to the realm of appearance, of play, of passing forms.

The search for the unchanging is not a rejection of life's movement, but a deeper inquiry: Is there something here that does not pass? Is there a ground beneath the shifting seasons, a witness that remains while all else comes and goes?

What cannot be broken?
What cannot be dissolved?
What cannot be surpassed?

The sages pointed to this as the essence of truth. It is not found in the leaves that fall, but in the tree that endures. Not in the ripples on the river's surface, but in the water itself. Not in the fleeting play of thoughts, but in the awareness in which they arise and vanish.

To see the changing as changing is wisdom. To discover the unchanging within it, is awakening. Imagine declaring, "This is true," only to watch it shift in the very next moment. What you called truth slips away. If truth is to be the foundation of existence, it cannot tremble with time.

What shifts belongs to appearance, not essence. What remains unchanged is the real.

The Illusion of Change

Everything seems to change. Faces age, bodies wrinkle, friendships bloom and fade. Mountains crumble into valleys, rivers shift their courses, stars collapse into darkness. On the surface, all is movement, all is impermanence.

And yet, when seen deeply, change touches only the surface.

- The ornament vanishes, yet gold remains.
- The wave collapses, yet the ocean abides.
- The dream dissolves, yet the dreamer still is.

Change is illusion not because it is unreal, but because it does not touch essence. The forms shift, but the substance endures. The names come and go, but the nameless remains untouched.

The sages remind us: the play is real as play, but not as ultimate truth. To mistake the ripple for the ocean, the costume for the actor, the shadow for the light, is illusion.

Change enchants us because it dances, dazzles, distracts. But behind the dance is the dancer who does not move. To know this is to see through the veil, not denying the play but no longer being deceived by it.

Substance and Form

Here lies a key distinction: form changes, essence does not.

Clay becomes a pot, a bowl, a statue. The shapes arise and disappear yet clay itself remains untouched.

Gold becomes rings, necklaces, coins. The ornaments shimmer, are worn, are melted down, yet gold abides.

A table may be painted, reshaped, or broken, but its essence, wood, defines its being. Change belongs to the outer garment. Essence is the body that wears it.

We mistake the garment for the being when we cling to form, forgetting the substance. We weep when the pot shatters, forgetting the clay is still here. We mourn the death of a form, forgetting the essence from which it rose has not been lost.

The world is a ceaseless parade of forms coming, going, rising and falling. But the one who sees deeply learns to look past the costume to the fabric, past the mask to the face, past the flickering image to the screen that never burns.

To know this distinction is to live in freedom. Forms may break, dissolve, vanish but essence cannot be touched.

Practice: Seeing Substance Beneath Form

Sit quietly for a few minutes. Let the body settle.

1. **Begin with the body.**

Notice your hands. They were once small and soft, now perhaps larger, stronger, or wrinkled. The form has changed again and again but has something constant carried through? Sense the aliveness underneath, the same life that was present in childhood, present now.

2. Move to thoughts.

Watch the stream of thoughts pass by. Each thought rises, lingers briefly, then dissolves. None remains. And yet, awareness, the space in which they appear has not changed. Thoughts are the clay pots; awareness is the clay.

3. Turn to feelings and relationships.

Consider love. Friends, partners, family may come and go, forms shifting like seasons. Yet the capacity to love, the essence of warmth and connection, remains steady beneath the forms it takes.

4. Rest in essence.

Let all forms, body, thoughts, emotions and memories, rise and fall without grasping. Then ask inwardly: What is here that does not come and go? Rest with that question, not rushing for an answer. Let the silence itself reveal.

The more we practice, the more forms are seen for what they are temporary garments. And slowly, attention begins to rest not in the garment but in the fabric itself, not in the pot but in the clay, not in the ornament but in the gold.

The Theater of Change

Consider the tomato.

Left on a counter, it rots in ten days and that feels normal, real. But what if it rotted in a single day? Or a single hour? Or a single second? The faster the change, the less real it feels. If it vanished in a blink, we would call it illusion.

This simple thought experiment reveals how our sense of "reality" is tied to the speed of change. Slow change feels solid, believable. Rapid change feels dreamlike, unreal. Yet the sages ask: why make this distinction at all? Why not see every change whether slow or fast as an illusion?

Much of what we call "truth" exists only because of memory. A face, a city, an event disappears once memory fades. They dissolve as though they never existed.

Dreams make this vivid. While dreaming, the world feels utterly real. Streets, voices, struggles, joy all feels convincing. But upon waking, the dream evaporates like mist. Where did it go? It was supported only by the mind.

So too with waking life: forms flicker, memory holds them briefly, and then they vanish. The unchanging essence alone remains.

And yet, in daily living, we cannot dismiss change. We eat food though it perishes. We ride trains though they rust. We tend our bodies though they age. Illusion is not useless; it is the very stage upon which the play of life unfolds. But when we seek ultimate truth, practical truths are not enough. We must look beneath the play into what does not come and go.

Life becomes more vibrant, not less, when impermanence is seen clearly. In fact, it grows lighter. For when you recognize that changing forms are only appearances, you do not grow cold or detached, you grow free.

The movie does not stop when you realize it is a movie. You still laugh, cry, and rejoice but without clinging, without fear. You play, knowing it is play.

This is the gift of seeing through the theater of change: to live fully in the drama of impermanence while resting in the stillness of the eternal. To dance with the forms yet never forget the essence.

Practice: Spotting the Unchanging

1. Sit quietly and notice something around you: a tree, a chair, your breath.
2. Ask: "What about these changes?" color, shape, form, feeling.
3. Then ask: "What remains constant beneath the change?"
   - The wood behind the table.
   - The clay behind the pot.
   - The awareness noticing it all.
4. Rest in that unchanging presence.
5. Slowly, the mind learns: change is the costume. The essence is always here, untouched.

Chapter 10

Ignorance: The Veil We Mistake for Knowledge

From Cluttered Certainty to the Openness of Innocence

The fog shouts loudly,
calling itself the sun.
But when the light rises,
fog was never real.

Ignorance is not simply the absence of knowledge. If it were merely "not knowing," it would be harmless, even innocent like an empty room waiting to be filled with light.

True ignorance is far more deceptive. It is not emptiness but clutter, a room so filled with junk that no light can enter. It is not just a gap in awareness, but the presence of wrong knowing. It is the tangle of beliefs, superstitions, assumptions, and half-digested ideas passed down through family, culture, and society. Ideas we never question because "everyone knows this is true." Illusions we guard fiercely because they give us comfort or identity.

Ignorance wears the mask of wisdom, but behind the mask there is no substance. And perhaps the most dangerous thing about ignorance is not its darkness but its arrogance. It does not whisper quietly, "I don't know." It shouts loudly, "I know!" It walks with the confidence of truth while being rooted in illusion.

This is why ignorance binds more tightly than emptiness. An empty mind can learn. The cluttered mind resists. The truly ignorant person is not the one who admits they do not know, but the one who refuses to question what they think they already know.

To begin the path of truth is not first to gather knowledge, but to sweep away false knowing, to clear the room so that the light can enter.

Recognizing the Signs of Ignorance

Ignorance is not always easy to see. It rarely comes to us wearing a sign that says "I am blindness." More often, it hides behind masks. It can sound clever, wear the robe of authority, or even speak with sincerity. That is why the seeker must learn to recognize its disguises, especially within themselves.

Here are some of its most common signs:

1. Blind Certainty

Ignorance loves certainty. It clings tightly to ideas, not because they are tested or true, but because they are familiar and comfortable. The louder the inner voice insists, "This must be true, and it cannot be questioned," the shakier the ground often is. Truth is steady but never rigid. It does not fear questions, it welcomes them. Just as a diamond does not lose its shine when examined, truth remains clear under scrutiny. Only illusions require force and rigidity to be maintained.

2. Defensiveness

Notice what happens when someone challenges your belief. Do you feel anger? Does your heart contract? Is your first instinct to defend rather than explore? If so, ignorance may be near. Truth is not afraid of inquiry. If what we believe is real, questions will only deepen our understanding. It is illusion that trembles under examination, like a shadow fleeing when light is brought close.

3. Inherited Beliefs

Much of what we call "knowledge" is borrowed from parents, culture, religion, or society. There is nothing wrong with receiving guidance, but when beliefs are never questioned, they become hand-me-down garments, worn simply because they were given to us. The seeker must ask honestly: "Do I know this from direct experience, or have I merely carried it because it was passed down?" Real wisdom is lived, not borrowed.

4. Fear of the Unknown

Ignorance fears mystery. It rushes to fill the unknown with quick assumptions, just to avoid the discomfort of not knowing. But the seeker must learn to stand in the openness of uncertainty. To remain with not-knowing is not weakness, it is the doorway to truth. A closed mind clings to conclusions; an open mind allows discovery.

5. Half-Digested Ideas

In today's age of endless information, ignorance often takes the form of fragments; a quote here, a headline there, a teaching half-understood. These scraps, when clung to without depth, create the illusion of wisdom while leaving the mind restless and shallow.

It is like eating raw ingredients without cooking them can be filling, perhaps, but not nourishing. True understanding comes only when ideas are digested, tested, lived, and absorbed into being. To see these signs in others is easy. To see them in ourselves requires great courage. Yet this courage is the true beginning of wisdom. For the moment you can say with humility, "Perhaps I do not know," a door opens.

Ignorance does not collapse through argument or attack. It dissolves through gentle seeing. Like shadows, it disappears when light is brought in.

Ignorance vs. Innocence

It is vital to distinguish between ignorance and innocence, for they may look similar on the surface but carry entirely different fragrances. Both may "not know," yet the quality of that not-knowing makes all the difference.

Innocence is open.

It is fresh, curious, like a child's gaze meeting the world for the first time. A child may not know the names of the stars, yet their eyes shine with wonder. This not-knowing is like a clear sky before dawn ready to welcome the first light of sunrise. Innocence is fertile soil. It can ripen into wisdom because it remains available, receptive, and alive.

Ignorance, by contrast, is closed.

It is not an empty sky, but one filled with dark clouds that block the light. Ignorance is heavy with borrowed beliefs, secondhand certainties, rigid assumptions. It does not say, "I do not know." Instead, it declares with pride, "I already know." In this way, ignorance shuts the very door through which learning could enter.

This is why the ignorant so often argue with great passion, not to discover truth, but to defend their fragile illusion of knowing. Their arguments are not a searchlight but a shield. They protect the ego's false security rather than expose it to the transforming fire of inquiry.

Innocence invites truth. Ignorance resists it. Innocence is soft, flexible, willing to be surprised. Ignorance is rigid, brittle, afraid of collapse. One is the seed of wisdom; the other is its greatest obstacle.

The seeker's task is not to collect knowledge to cover their ignorance, but to recover the lost openness of innocence. For when the mind becomes like a child again, fresh, uncluttered, unafraid of not-knowing, wisdom enters naturally, like sunlight through an open window.

How Ignorance is Born

No one consciously chooses ignorance. No child is born saying, “I wish to be blind.” Ignorance grows slowly, silently, like weeds in the soil of our upbringing. It is not a deliberate choice but an unconscious inheritance.

From the moment we arrive, the world begins to shape us. Family traditions whisper their certainties. Education offers facts, some true, others partial. Religion provides dogmas, rituals, and beliefs. Media floods the senses with images and narratives. Politics weaves its stories of identity and division. Without awareness, we absorb it all like sponges.

Some of what we take in is nourishing, some poisonous, and much of its half-true fragments of reality bent by perspective, culture, or convenience. But in the tender soil of the child’s mind, all seeds sprout alike. We cannot yet tell wisdom from superstition, clarity from distortion.

Over time, these seeds harden into unquestioned “truths.” We grow not only with them but within them. They become the walls of the house in which the mind resides. And soon, we forget that the house was built at all. We think its walls are the world itself.

The mind clings to these beliefs not because they are necessarily true, but because they feel safe.

To question them would be to question the ground beneath our feet.

For what happens if I discover that everything, I believed about myself, about others, about the world, is false? Who am I then? Where do I stand?

That fear is what keeps ignorance alive. Not ignorance itself, but the terror of losing the scaffolding it provides. To step outside the inherited walls feels like stepping into emptiness. And so most prefer the comfort of illusion to the vastness of the unknown.

But truth can only be found by those willing to risk this step. By those willing to let false ground crumble so the real ground may be discovered. Ignorance is born of fear, but wisdom is born of courage.

How Ignorance is Sustained

Ignorance, once born, does not remain weak or fragile. It grows roots, learns to defend itself, and becomes clever at survival. What begins as a single unexamined idea can grow into a fortress of conviction. Like ivy clinging to stone, it wraps tightly around the mind until even light struggles to enter.

How does ignorance sustain itself?

1. Habit

The first fuel of ignorance is repetition. What we hear and repeat often begins to feel like truth, even without foundation. A phrase spoken a hundred times sounds more convincing than one tested once.

This is why old sayings, prejudices, and assumptions linger, they are familiar. And the mind, mistaking familiarity for reality, confuses repetition with truth. Like a well-worn path in the forest, the more it is walked, the harder it is to imagine another way.

2. Social Reinforcement

Ignorance is rarely solitary. It is often collective, carried by families, communities, and cultures across generations. "This is how things are," people say, without question.

To challenge these beliefs can feel dangerous. To question what everyone else accepts risks ridicule, conflict, or even exile. And so many remain silent, choosing belonging over clarity. Ignorance, in this way, is not sustained by evidence but by the deep human need for acceptance.

3. Pride

Once we declare something as truth, our ego resists letting go. To say "I was wrong" feels like admitting weakness, even death, to the mind that builds its identity around knowledge.

This pride becomes a guard at the gate, refusing correction even when evidence knocks loudly. How many wars, arguments, and broken relationships have continued not because truth was unclear, but because pride would not

allow, "I was mistaken."

4. Fear of Change

At its root, ignorance survives because truth is disruptive. Seeing clearly may demand a change in lifestyle, identity, or worldview. It may require courage, humility, or surrender.

Sometimes the mind senses that clarity would unravel the old comfort, the old story, the old self. And so, it clings to illusion, preferring the safety of the familiar over the unsettling light of truth. In this way, ignorance feels easier like staying in a dark room rather than stepping into the brightness that blinds at first.

5. The Illusion of Knowing

Perhaps the most dangerous sustainer of ignorance is the belief that we already know. The moment the mind says, "I have all the answers," learning stops. The moment the heart says, "I understand fully," listening ends.

This false confidence shuts the door, even while wisdom patiently knocks. Like a traveler who mistakes a map for the destination, the illusion of knowing keeps us from walking further.

Ignorance is not sustained by darkness alone, but by our own resistance to light. Like a dream, it continues until someone dares to awaken.

To dismantle ignorance, the seeker must cultivate the opposite:

- **Curiosity** instead of habit.
- **Courage** instead of fear.
- **Humility** instead of pride.
- **Openness** instead of rigidity.

Ignorance thrives on closed doors. Wisdom enters only through open ones

The Consequences of Ignorance

Ignorance is not harmless. It is costly both personally and collectively. Left unexamined, it becomes the unseen hand that shapes our lives and our world.

On the individual level, ignorance appears as confusion, a mind unable to discern what is real from what is illusion. It leads to impulsive choices that bring regret, to addictions that promise relief but deepen suffering, to fragile egos that mask insecurity with loud declarations of certainty. A life lived in ignorance is a life lived in shadows, chasing images instead of substance.

On the collective level, ignorance multiplies its damage. When enough individuals are blind, entire societies stumble. Ignorance gives birth to wars fought over illusions, to exploitation of the weak by the powerful, to inequality justified by untested dogmas, to blind obedience in the face of corruption. A population that cannot think, question, or see clearly can be easily manipulated and history is filled with the scars of such blindness.

In short, ignorance is expensive. It costs us clarity, it costs us peace, and it costs us freedom. It robs humanity of its highest potential, binding us to cycles of suffering that need not continue.

Recognizing Ignorance in Ourselves

The first step in dissolving ignorance is the hardest: to see it within ourselves. For ignorance does not like to be exposed. It wears masks, it argues, it defends. Yet there are red flags, subtle but consistent that signal its presence.

- **Resistance to new ideas.** The unwillingness to even consider another perspective is a hallmark of ignorance. Truth has nothing to fear from exploration.
- **Arguing to win, not to learn.** When the goal of discussion is victory rather than discovery, the ego is speaking, not wisdom.
- **Confusion and contradiction.** A mind that clings to illusion often collapses under its own weight. When ideas do not cohere, it is a sign the foundation is weak.
- **Blind belief in authority.** Accepting something as true merely because it was said by a teacher, leader, or book without testing, is ignorance disguised as loyalty.
- **Fear of being wrong.** The deeper the fear of error, the more tightly ignorance grips. A wise mind is not afraid of being wrong, for every error revealed is a step closer to clarity.

Each of these is a mirror held up to the self, revealing the mind's attachment to illusion. To recognize these signs is already to weaken ignorance. Awareness is the beginning of freedom.

The Compassionate View

It is easy to grow impatient with the ignorant. To watch someone, cling stubbornly to illusion can stir frustration, even anger. Yet the seeker must remember: the ignorant is not bad, only asleep. Their blindness is not born of malice, but of conditioning. Just as a child repeats the words they hear at home, the adult repeats the beliefs absorbed from family, culture, and society.

And the same applies to us. Whenever ignorance within us is exposed, the temptation is to condemn ourselves, to feel shame or guilt. But condemnation only deepens the darkness. What frees is gentleness. To meet our ignorance with curiosity rather than judgment. To say: "Ah, here is a blind spot I had not seen. How wonderful that it is now revealed."

Compassion turns ignorance from an enemy into a teacher. Each illusion uncovered is a doorway, an opening through which wisdom can enter. Where there is compassion, even ignorance becomes a stepping stone.

The Way Out of Ignorance

Escaping ignorance does not mean piling up endless facts or memorizing more information. It means cultivating clarity, a way of seeing that cut through illusion like a lamp in darkness.

- **Awareness:** The first step is humility, to admit, "I may not know." This simple acknowledgment cracks the shell of arrogance and allows light to enter.
- **Questioning:** The seeker must ask, "Is this really true? How do I know?" Each question chips away at illusion, loosening what was once tightly held.
- **Direct Experience:** Truth reveals itself in living contact. To test, to taste, to see with one's own eyes dissolves secondhand belief and anchors knowledge in reality.
- **Guidance:** A teacher, a wise friend, or even the words of a book can hold up a mirror to what we cannot see ourselves. Guidance does not replace our seeing, but it points the way toward it.

The journey out of ignorance requires courage. The courage to let go of false comforts, the courage to step naked into the unknown. Yet in this very act of letting go, we discover the ground we feared was missing.

For beyond ignorance, beyond illusion, lies not emptiness, but the vast and luminous simplicity of truth.

Conclusion: A Lifelong Unveiling

Ignorance is not a defect. It is not a flaw to be ashamed of. It is the shared beginning of every human journey. To be born is to begin in darkness; to walk the path is to slowly let light in. The true mistake is not being ignorant but refusing to see it, refusing to allow the possibility that what we hold as truth may in fact be illusion.

Even the wisest are ignorant about something. The difference is not that they "know everything," but that they carry their ignorance lightly. They do not cling to the illusion of certainty. They have learned the sacred art of humility, the ability to bow before the vastness and say: "I don't know. But I am willing to see, to learn, to be surprised."

This humility is not weakness. It is strength. It is the openness in which learning never ends, and therefore wisdom never stagnates. For wisdom is not a possession but a living stream, always flowing, always fresh.

The more we learn, the more we realize how little we truly know. Yet this does not make us insecure; it makes us free. It frees us from the burden of needing to have all the answers, from the prison of defending illusions. It allows us to live in wonder, to rest in the mystery, to move with life's unfolding rather than against it.

In this vast openness, ignorance cannot breathe. Its walls collapse, its shadows dissolve. What remains is awareness, which is clear, spacious and luminous. And from that awareness, wisdom blooms like a lotus opening to the sun.

Ignorance is the beginning, but not the end. The journey is a lifelong unveiling, each step peeling away illusion, each moment offering a chance to see more clearly. And in that unveiling, we discover that truth was never far away. It was always here, shining quietly behind the veil.

Ignorance is shadow, wisdom is light.

To say "I know" is to close,
to say "I don't know" is to open.

The more I learn,
the vaster the unknown.
The vaster the unknown,
the freer I am.

Meditation: Watching Ignorance

1. Sit quietly and recall a time you argued with someone.
2. Ask: "Was I seeking truth, or defending my 'rightness'?"
3. Notice the energy of ignorance, tight, fearful, rigid.
4. Now recall a moment of genuine curiosity. Notice its openness, lightness, and freedom.
5. Rest in that openness. That is the seed of wisdom.

Chapter 11

The Freedom of Unknowing

When Wisdom Flowers as Silence

The wise sit smiling,
cup empty, hands open.
Nothing to hold,
and so, everything is held.

On the path of knowledge, there comes a strange and humbling moment. You pause and see that all you thought you "knew" was never truth, but only reflections, illusions dressed in the garments of certainty. Beliefs, memories, experiences, each seemed solid, yet each dissolve when examined closely. They are shadows on a wall, flickering and fading, never the light itself.

This is the root of ignorance: not the absence of knowing, but the mistaking of shadows for substance. To cling to the flickering play of experience and declare it absolute is to build a house upon sand.

The greatest illusion of all is the belief in separation. We assume: “I am this body, born at this time, destined to die in a few decades.” Around this fragile idea, we construct the whole architecture of life, survival, ambition, desire, and fear. Yet this very assumption of limitation is the seed of suffering. The moment you say, “I am small, I am separate, I am finite,” life becomes a desperate struggle against time. Every joy is shadowed by the fear of loss. Every success tremble under the certainty of ending.

The path of wisdom does not add more bricks to this fragile house. It does not pile more facts upon the shaky foundation. Instead, it asks a radical question: “Who is the ‘I’ that believes itself separate?” When this assumption is dissolved, suffering loses its root.

Wisdom begins not in accumulation, but in unlearning. Not in certainty, but in surrender. Not in adding, but in dissolving. What remains when illusion falls away is not emptiness, but fullness, a vastness that has no beginning and no end.

The Paradox of Knowledge

We are taught that knowledge is the light that clears ignorance. And in a sense, it is true. Knowledge shows us the errors of belief, the cracks in illusion, the patterns hidden beneath appearances. But look deeper, and the paradox reveals itself: all knowledge is born of experience.

And if experience itself is fleeting, shifting, dream-like, then knowledge, too, is only part of the dream.

Strange, isn't it? The very tool we depend on to escape illusion is itself woven out of illusion. Like trying to climb out of a dream using the dream's own ladders, we soon realize that every step upward is still within the dream.

So, what then? Do we abandon knowledge? Not quite. We use it but as one uses a thorn to remove a thorn. Knowledge is not for collecting, but for peeling away, layer by layer, every falsehood. Each concept tested, each belief examined, each veil lifted. And at the end of the peeling, nothing new is added. Nothing is gained. What remains is not "more knowledge," but the clear, empty mirror itself, silent, still, radiant.

The Desert Mirage

Imagine standing in a vast desert, parched with thirst. On the horizon, a shimmering lake appears. With hope renewed, you walk toward it. Yet no matter how close you come, it slips farther away. Finally, in exhaustion, you see clearly there was never water, only a mirage.

So, it is with knowledge. We chase it with eagerness, gathering books, collecting teachings, polishing ideas. But as we draw closer, the substance dissolves. The words cannot quench the thirst, the concepts cannot nourish the soul. In the end, you realize: there was never "truth" to possess, never "knowledge" to hold. The mirage itself was the teacher, guiding you not to quench thirst, but to see through illusion. The secret then is this: the path of knowledge is, in truth, the path of unknowing.

A Journey of Reduction

In the world, learning is measured by accumulation, more facts, more skills, more achievements. The bookshelf grows, the certificates pile up, the identity of "knower" swells with pride.

But the deeper path is the opposite. Real knowledge is not addition but subtraction. With each step forward, something false falls away: a superstition, a prejudice, a borrowed belief, a concept mistaken for truth. You do not grow heavier, you grow lighter. You do not become someone who "knows everything," but someone who is free of the burden of false knowing.

And in the end, what do you hold? Nothing.

But that nothing is not empty, it is fullness itself. It is the wide sky when the clouds dissolve, the mirror when the dust is wiped away. That nothing is freedom, silence, wholeness. That nothing is everything.

The Edge of the Mind

The mind is a brilliant tool, endlessly clever yet inevitably limited. It can arrange concepts like a craftsman stacking stones. It can compare patterns, weave philosophies, and construct entire worlds of thought. But when it comes face-to-face with reality itself, naked, unmediated, unspeakable, the mind falters. It stutters, trembles, and finally falls silent.

At the core of existence, there are no concepts, no words, no philosophies. There is only the silent, luminous fact of being. Pure presence without label, without division. Here, the cleverness of the mind bows. It cannot cross this threshold.

And in that bowing, a new fragrance arises, the fragrance of peace.

The Mystic's Paradox

Standing at this edge, the seeker encounters a strange and wondrous paradox. You know because ignorance has been stripped away. Yet at the same time, you know that you do not know because truth itself cannot be captured in the nets of thought. This is the mystic's state: to walk in both knowing and unknowing at once. It is the freedom of the agnostic in its truest sense, not the skeptic's denial, but the courage to admit: "I don't know." Not as weakness, but as clarity. For those who claim, "I know everything," are lost in arrogance, trapped in illusion. But the one who says, "I don't know," with awareness, stands at the doorway of truth.

Here, knowledge bows into wonder. Thought dissolves into silence. And silence reveals more than all the libraries of the world.

The Freedom of Unknowing

The one who embraces unknowing is free. They no longer carry the heavy armor of ideology, no longer need to defend dogma, no longer cling to the brittle pride of certainty. They live lightly, breathe openly, and question deeply. Their strength lies not in having all the answers, but in resting comfortably in the vastness of the unanswered. Ask them for their philosophy, and they may laugh: "None." Ask them what they know, and they may smile gently: "I don't know."

This is not ignorance. It is wisdom flowering as humility, awareness ripening into wonder. To rest in unknowing is to rest in life's mystery without fear. It is to let the heart be spacious enough to hold paradox, silence, and infinite possibility.

In such a state, truth is no longer a concept to be grasped — it is a presence to be lived.

Conclusion: The Peace of the Empty Cup

The journey of knowledge does not end in a grand library, stacked with answers to every question. It ends in an empty cup. And paradoxically, it is this emptiness that makes the cup ready for the infinite.

The agnostic, the mystic, the true seeker, they all arrive here, at the quiet edge of knowing. They discover that the ultimate truth is beyond the grasp of words, beyond the reach of concepts, beyond the nets of the mind. And yet, instead of despair, they find joy. Instead of fear, they find freedom.

Unknowing is not a failure, but a flowering. It is the final liberation from the burden of needing certainty, from the restless compulsion to grasp and define. In the peace of unknowing, the seeker dissolves into the vastness itself.

Here, knowledge has served its purpose. It has led you to the shore, but it cannot carry you across. To step beyond is to step into silence, into mystery, into the infinite embrace of being.

This is the secret of the empty cup: when nothing is held, everything can pour in. When all knowing is released, truth reveals itself, not as an object to be possessed, but as the very essence of life lived in freedom.

Unknowing is not the end of the path. It is the arrival. It is not emptiness to be feared, but spaciousness to be loved. In it, the seeker rests, not with answers, but with peace.

Meditation: Resting in Unknowing

1. Sit quietly. Let every belief, every idea, every certainty drift away.
2. Whisper to yourself gently: "I don't know."
3. Feel the openness this creates: spacious, limitless.
4. Rest in that openness, without trying to fill it.
5. Notice: the peace of unknowing is far greater than the burden of knowing.

Chapter 12

Existence: The Silent Companion

The Mystery That Always Is

No beginning, no end.
No inside, no outside.
No question, no answer.
Only the quiet fact: I Am.

Existence, a vast and mysterious word, yet the simplest of truths. It is the hum beneath every breath, the silent presence behind every thought, the still ground beneath every step. Before the mind can ask "Why?" or "How?", existence has already answered: "Here."

We spend our days chasing fragments, people, plans, problems, pleasures. Our eyes dart toward what changes, while the changeless slips quietly by. And yet, all along, existence remains like the canvas beneath a painting, the stage beneath the play, the silence after the final note of a song. Rarely do we pause to notice it. Rarely do we bow to its simplicity. For the mind seeks complication, while existence is simplicity itself.

And here lies the most beautiful discovery: Existence is not many. It is not divided. It is not scattered into fragments. Existence is one. The same presence that looks through your eyes beats through the heart of the stars. The same stillness that rests in your silence vibrates in the silence of the forest, the ocean, the night sky.

Let us, then, wander gently, curiously, playfully through the questions of existence. Not as riddles to be solved, but as doorways into wonder. Not to capture truth, but to fall in love with it.

What is Existence?

Existence is everything.

The stars overhead burning in silence, the ache that lingers in your shoulder, the first cry of a newborn, the dream that dissolved when you wake up, all of it belongs inside the Existence and nothing stands outside its embrace. Even your questions about existence, your doubts, your denials too are already within it.

Existence is so vast that it includes even illusion. It does not reject the false; it simply contains it. Like the wide sky that welcomes both storm clouds and radiant blue, existence holds truth and untruth, shadow and light, joy and sorrow. It allows them to pass through, but it is not bound by them.

Think of it: even when you say, “This cannot be,” you affirm existence, for your disbelief itself exists. Even when you dream, your dream exists within the larger field of being. Existence is the stage, the actors, the play, and the silence after the curtain falls.

It is whole. It is seamless. It is complete. And the greatest wonder is this: you are not outside of it, seeking your way in. You are already it, breathing, sensing, thinking. To ask "What is existence?" is itself existence questioning itself. The question and the answer rise and fall in the same boundless ocean.

Why Does It Exist?

This is the child's question, the philosopher's puzzle, the mystic's wonder: Why is there something rather than nothing? And yet, the most honest answer is silence. Existence does not carry a reason in its pocket. It is not a project with a goal, not a story with a moral, not an invention with a function. It is not the kind of thing that needs a "why."

A flower blooms without reason. A bird sings without purpose. A river flows without asking why it flows. Likewise, existence simply is.

Even the question, why? arises within it. You cannot stand outside of existence to interrogate it. The question is already part of the very mystery it seeks to solve.

Perhaps the better question is not "Why does it exist?" but "Can I sit quietly in its presence?"

How Did It Begin?

It didn't.

There is no "before" existence, just as there is nothing "north" of the North Pole. Beginning and ending are ideas that make sense only within existence. They belong to the realm of appearances, not to the ground itself.

When a child is born, we call it a beginning. When a star collapses, we call it an ending. But both happen within the boundless ocean of being, which itself does not start or stop.

The ocean does not "begin" when a wave rises, nor does it "end" when a wave falls. So too, existence abides while all forms arise and pass away.

When Did It Start?

Never. Existence is timeless.

Clocks tick. Calendars flip. Histories unfold. But these belong to the play, not to the stage. Time is a costume existence wears. A rhythm that helps the dance unfold. But existence itself does not tick. It does not age. It does not move from past to future.

It is the eternal now in which all pasts and futures appear, like clouds drifting across an endless sky. When you stop chasing memory and anticipation, you glimpse it: the ever-present fact of being.

Where Is It?

Everywhere. And nowhere.

Point anywhere, a city, a forest, the moon, your own beating heart. All are existence. Nothing you touch can fall outside of it.

Yet existence itself has no fixed address. It cannot be located on a map, cannot be pinned down to coordinates. Places exist within it, but it has no place of its own.

It is the groundless ground in which all locations arise and vanish. Like space itself, containing everything but contained by nothing, existence has no edge.

Who Is Existence?

This is perhaps the most persistent mistake: imagining existence as a "someone."

Existence is not a king on a throne, not a cosmic engineer, not a person with preferences and plans. It has no face, no gender, no name. Personalities arise within it, like sparks in a fire, but existence itself is impersonal, vast, free and ungraspable.

Yet paradoxically, it is also intimate. The same vast existence that stretches into galaxies is looking out through your eyes, breathing through your lungs, pulsing through your veins.

It is not a "who," but it is what you are.

How Many Existences Are There?

Only one.

It dances as many: mountain, cloud, man, woman, child, bird, river, star. To the senses, it appears as countless forms. But the essence is indivisible.

The many is the One in costume. A thousand waves, one ocean. A thousand ornaments, one gold. A thousand words, one silence.

When you see only the forms, you see difference. When you see through the forms, you recognize the One playing as many.

Is Existence True or False?

Both: and neither.

A dream feels true while you dream it. Upon waking, you call it false. But even the dream existed. It arose, it played and it vanished.

So too with waking life: some experiences are "real," others prove to be illusions. Yet both belong to existence.

Existence is not bound by the game of true and false. It holds them the way the sky holds clouds and blue without preference, without attachment. It simply is.

Reflection: The Silent Companion

When the mind asks these questions: why, how, when, where, who, how many, true or false, it eventually runs into silence. And in that silence, something astonishing is seen: existence has been here all along, quietly, patiently, without need of defense. It does not argue, it does not explain, it does not justify itself. It simply offers itself in every breath, every sound, every sensation.

To live in tune with this is to walk lightly, to act with clarity, and to rest in peace. Existence becomes not an object to understand, but a silent companion to be trusted.

In the end, the truest answer to every question about existence is not a word, but a pause, a quiet bow to the mystery that always was, always is, and always will be.

Practices for Savoring Existence

1. **Sky-Gazing**

Look up at the sky. Notice how it holds clouds, birds, planes, and weather, yet remains vast and untouched. Now imagine existence as this sky: everything arises within it, but it is never disturbed.

2. **The "Why?" Pause**

Next time you ask "Why me? Why this? Why now?": pause. Smile at the mind's hunger for reasons. Then whisper softly: Existence is reasonless. Let that freedom settle in your chest.

3. **Timelessness Practice**

Close your eyes. Forget clocks, forget past and future, just for a minute. Rest in what is here, now. Notice: existence has no beginning or end.

4. **One or Many?**

Pick up an object nearby, a cup of tea, a pen, a stone. Ask: "Is this separate, or is it existence wearing a costume?" Let the playfulness ripple through you.

5. **The "Who Am I?" Flip**

Instead of asking, "Who am I?", ask, "Who is existence?" Notice that it is not a person, but the totality in which your sense of self arises.

Existence is not a puzzle. It is a mystery. Not to be solved, but to be sipped like tea. Sit with it as you would with a dear friend. Quietly. Lovingly. Let it surprise you, again and again.

Chapter 13

The Open Secret of Emptiness

The Womb of Existence and the Freedom of No-Self

A cup holds water only because it is empty.
A window lets in light only because it is clear.
A note becomes music only because silence surrounds it.
A wave rises only because the ocean is free to move.

Emptiness is not the absence of life. It is the space in which life blooms. We spend our lives chasing fullness. Full shelves, full calendars, full bellies, full minds. We equate fullness with value. But look more closely, the greatest treasures in life are valuable not because of their fullness, but because of their emptiness.

Beyond Nothingness

When people first hear the word "emptiness," they recoil. It sounds bleak, hollow, cold, a void of despair. But the sages were not pointing to nothingness. They were pointing to openness.

Emptiness does not mean "nothing exists." It means nothing exists as a separate, fixed essence. Everything leans on everything else.

A tree is not just a tree. It is also soil, water, sunlight, air, and time woven together. Remove one, and the tree cannot stand.

You, too, are not separate. You are breath from the forest, warmth from the sun, nourishment from the earth, love from countless others. Everything is dependent. Everything is interwoven. Everything is fluid.

This is emptiness: the absence of a solid "self," the absence of separateness. And in that absence lies infinite possibility. Because nothing is fixed, everything can change. Because no form is permanent, every form is free to dance.

The Movie and the Screen

Think of a cinema. The lights dim, the movie begins, and suddenly you are swept into another world. For two hours, you cry, laugh, love, and fear with the characters. The story feels real. And yet, what is it all? Only patterns of light projected onto a blank screen. Life, too, is like this. The drama of forms, relationships, ambitions, nations, successes and failures, feels utterly real. And it is, in its way. But behind it all is the vast screen of emptiness: the silent presence that allows every story to be projected yet remains untouched.

Without the screen, there is no movie.
Without emptiness, there is no existence.

The secret is this: the movie is not false. It is a play. The screen is not opposed to it. It makes the play possible.

The Ocean of Change

Look at the waves. Each rise, peaks, crashes, dissolves. To the casual eye, each wave seems unique, separate, solid. But what are they made of? Nothing but the ocean itself.

The wave is born, dances for a while, and dies. The ocean abides.

This is the great metaphor of life. Every event, every feeling, everybody is a wave. Born, moving, dissolving. Beneath them, the ocean of emptiness holds all, vast, fluid and open.

Emptiness is not a barren void. It is the womb of the world. It births forms, takes them back, and births again. Every tear, every laugh, every star, every world is a wave upon this endless ocean of potential.

Emptiness as Freedom

Why does this matter for us? Because once you see that nothing is fixed, you are free.

- No failure is final.
- No identity is absolute.
- No belief needs to imprison you.

The roles you play as parent, worker, seeker, friend, are costumes. Beautiful and meaningful, but not ultimate. The tightest knots in your life are only temporary weavings of conditions. Change the conditions, and the knot loosens.

This realization is not bleak. It is liberation. You are no longer a prisoner of the story. You are the space in which stories arise.

To see emptiness is to taste freedom.

The Dance of Existence and Emptiness

Existence and emptiness are not two. They are two faces of the same mystery.

Existence says: Everything is.
Emptiness says: Nothing is fixed.

Together, they whisper: Dance. Live. Laugh. Don't cling too tightly.

When you grasp existence without emptiness, life feels heavy as a burden of permanence. When you grasp emptiness without existence, life feels hollow, a negation. But when you see both together, life becomes light like a play, a festival or a dance.

The wave does not deny its rising and falling. But it knows, in its depth, that it is the ocean.

Living the Secret

When you live this secret, the world changes. You still drink tea, care for loved ones, feel pain, celebrate joy. The movie continues. But your heart is lighter. You no longer cling to the characters or fear the ending, because you know the screen.

You can play fully, cry deeply, laugh loudly and yet rest in the silent ground beneath it all. This is the open secret of emptiness: It does not strip life of meaning. It makes life boundless. It does not deny existence. It reveals its depth.

When this truth sinks in, life is no longer a desperate clinging to passing waves, but a joyful dance of forms upon the vast ocean of potential.

Practice: Tasting Emptiness

1. Close your eyes. Notice a thought. Watch as it vanishes.
2. Feel an emotion calm, restless, excited, anxious. Notice how it shifts.
3. Watch your breath, each one comes, each one goes.
4. Behind all of this movement, notice the still space that allows it.
5. Rest in that openness. That is emptiness, alive with possibility.

Workbook: A 7-Day Journey into Existence & Emptiness

Day 1: Sipping Existence

- **Theme:** Everything is.
- **Practice:** Sit quietly. Whisper inside, I exist. Then drop the "I" and rest in Existence is.
- **Playful Twist:** Point to a random object (coffee, cat, pen) and say: Existence is playing as this.

- **Reflections:** How does it feel to shift from "I exist" to "Existence is"? Did anything feel more alive?

Day 2: Where Is It?

- **Theme:** Existence has no location.
- **Practice:** Sense space around you. Notice it's not "here" or "there."
- **Playful Twist:** Point randomly like a child and shout: Existence!
- **Reflections:** What happens when you drop the idea that existence is "somewhere"?

Day 3: Timeless Being

- **Theme:** No beginning or end.
- **Practice:** Try to catch the first moment of "now." Spoiler: you can't.
- **Playful Twist:** Giggle at how "now" keeps slipping through your fingers.
- **Reflections:** Did this change your sense of urgency or time?

Day 4: The Empty Cup

- **Theme:** Emptiness is possibility.
- **Practice:** Hold an empty cup. See how emptiness makes it useful.
- **Playful Twist:** Offer the cup to the universe and whisper, fill me with whatever you like.

- **Reflections:** How is emptiness different from "nothing"?

Day 5: Watching the Movie

- **Theme:** Life is appearance.
- **Practice:** Watch thoughts as movie scenes. Notice the screen remains.
- **Playful Twist:** Say once today, I'm watching the greatest movie ever, called Life.
- **Reflections:** Did this make your thoughts lighter?

Day 6: Ocean & Waves

- **Theme:** Change is movement, not substance.
- **Practice:** Imagine yourself as the ocean. Emotions = waves.
- **Playful Twist:** Next time you're emotional, say, just another wave in the ocean of me.
- **Reflections:** Did this soften your relationship with strong emotions?

Day 7: The Great Mystery

- **Theme:** The unknowable is most intimate.
- **Practice:** Drop all questions. Rest in the mystery: Existence is.
- **Playful Twist:** Laugh at the absurdity: you'll never figure it out, and that's the beauty.
- **Reflections:** Did the mystery feel scary, peaceful, or playful?

Closing Invitation

Do not think of this as the end of a workbook, but the beginning of a way of seeing.

You have walked through fullness and emptiness. Through being and becoming.

Not to collect knowledge, but to relax into what already is.

Emptiness is not the absence of life. It is the infinite potential of life, waiting to surprise you.

Chapter 14

The Silent Witness

Awareness Beyond Experiencer and Experience

The river flows.
The leaves rustle.
The mind weaves its endless tapestry.
Yet beneath it all,
silent, still, unseen,
the witness remains.
Not the river,
not the leaf,
not the mind.
But that which knows them all,
without ever moving.
Look closely...
you will not find it.
And yet without it,
nothing could be found.
Rest here,
in the quiet light
that sees without being seen.

We have spoken of existence as vast, infinite, and unknowable. But to step closer, let us draw a playful line not as ultimate truth, but as a way of seeing. On one side lies that which appears: the endless stream of experience. A sound arises, a thought drifts by, a sensation glows in the body, an emotion passes like weather. All of these belong to the flow of appearance, fleeting, ever-changing, never still. On the other side lies that which knows the appearing: the quiet witness, awareness itself. It does not come and go. It simply receives.

This division, of course, is not ultimately real. It is like drawing a line across the open sky, useful for orientation, but the sky itself remains seamless. Experience and experiencer are never apart; they rise together, inseparable, as flame and light, wave and water, dance and dancer. And yet, by playing with this distinction, something profound is revealed.

When you turn your attention to the appearing, you notice its restlessness: forms flicker, thoughts dissolve, sensations shift. But when you turn toward the one who knows, you encounter a mystery. The experiencer cannot be seen as an object, cannot be touched or described. It is not a thought, not a memory, not a sensation. It is the open space in which all of these unfold. Searching for it is like looking for your glasses while already wearing them. The very act of searching hides the truth.

And here lies the hidden doorway: you begin to see that you are not merely the appearances, not merely the experiencer, but the luminous field in which both arise together. The distinction collapses, and what remains is the simple, unbroken fact of being, effortless, vast, and whole.

The Experiencer Cannot Be Experienced

The experiencer forever slips through the fingers of grasping. You can point to a mountain, and there it stands. You can describe the fragrance of a flower, and it is recalled. You can replay a memory and watch its images flicker. But the experiencer? It cannot be pointed at, because it is the very light by which pointing, recalling, perceiving happens.

It is not an object. It cannot be touched, for it is the touch itself. It cannot be heard, for it is the background silence in which every sound appears. It cannot be remembered, for even memory rises in it and vanishes back into it. The experiencer is not in time. Time itself is known because of it.

Advaita or Nonduality philosophy calls this - the witness, the pure awareness. Like the eye that sees but cannot see itself, the witness reveals all things yet is never revealed as a "thing." Whatever you can observe, thought, body, emotion, perception, is not the experiencer. For the simple reason: it is observed. The witness is that which knows, never what is known. The mind resists this truth, for it always wants to hold, to frame, to possess. But the experiencer is too close to be grasped. It is nearer than your own heartbeat, nearer than the thought "I am," nearer than the one who says "near." It is so intimate that you overlook it, like a wave asking, "Where is the ocean?"

You say, "I see." Who is this "I" that sees? You say, "I hear." Who is this "I" that hears? Whatever is known cannot be the knower. Peel away the layers, and only the luminous knowing itself remains, ungraspable, unchanging, unbound.

The experiencer cannot be experienced. Yet without it, no experience is possible. It is not something you gain; it is what you already are. To "realize" it is not to add something new, but to drop the false notion that it was ever absent.

This is the essence of non-dual philosophy: the seeker and the sought are never two. The very awareness searching for truth is the truth itself. When this is seen, the search collapses into stillness. Nothing more needs to be added, nothing more needs to be attained.

The play of life continues, thoughts, sensations, desires, fears, seasons, stories, but all arise and dissolve in the same open presence. That presence is untouched. That presence is you.

The Self-Illumined Nature

How do we know the experiencer is real? Because experience itself is undeniable. You may question everything, the world outside, the body, even the mind, but you cannot deny the simple fact that you are aware. Wherever there is experience, there must be those who experience. Awareness does not need to be proven; its very presence is the proof.

This is why the sages call it self-illumined. Objects need something outside them to be known, a flower needs light to be seen, a sound needs ears to be heard, a thought needs the mind to recognize it. But awareness needs nothing else to reveal it. It shines by its very being. It is not revealed through experience, but as the background of every experience.

The Upanishads ask: "By what shall you know That, by which all this is known?" The experiencer cannot be shown by another, because it is already the showing itself. Just as the sun does not require a torch to prove that it is shining, awareness needs no validation. Its existence is self-evident, woven into every perception, every thought, every doubt, every dream.

Even ignorance testifies to it. To say “I don’t know” already proves the one who knows the not-knowing. Even sleep, in which objects vanish, still leaves a trace, “I slept well.” Who reports this if not awareness, present even in absence? Thus, the witness is not a conclusion, but a fact so intimate, so close, that it is constantly overlooked.

This is the meaning of self-illumination. Awareness does not need another awareness to be aware of it. It is its own light. It shines not on itself as an object, but as the subject that makes all objects possible. You cannot see it, but without it, no seeing would ever happen. You cannot touch it, but without it, no touch would be known. You cannot remember it as a thing, but without it, no memory could arise at all.

The experiencer is the light behind all lights, the witness behind all appearances. To awaken to this is not to acquire something new, but to recognize what has always been silently shining at the heart of your being.

The Unity of Experiencer and Experience

Does the experiencer come first, or the experience? The question itself dissolves when looked at deeply. They are not two separate entities, waiting in line for one to precede the other. They arise together, inseparable, like the wave and the ocean, like fire and its warmth. No experiencer without experience, and no experience without experiencer. They are twin aspects of one reality.

Think of a mirror and its reflections. The mirror does not wait for reflections, nor do reflections exist apart from the mirror. They are not two, though we speak of them as if they were. So, it is with experiencer and experience. We imagine a subject here and an object there, but in truth they bloom together, in the same instant, as the very dance of awareness. The experiencer is like the silent screen, vast and unmoving. Experience is the play of colors, shapes, and stories dancing upon it. Yet unlike cinema, there is no reel to run out, no projector to switch off, no final credits rolling into silence. This play is beginningless and endless, an eternal unfolding without a first frame and without a last.

To seek which came first is to miss the point. The two are not separate strands woven later into a fabric; they are the fabric itself. Subject and object, knower and known, witness and witnessed, they are distinctions made by the mind, useful in language, but not real in essence. In the direct seeing of Advaita, this becomes luminous: the one who sees and what is seen are not-two. The sound and the hearer, the thought and the thinker, the breath and the breather, all appear as a single movement in the vastness of awareness.

And yet, awareness itself, the screen, remains untouched. Just as fire is not burned by its own flame, the experiencer is not altered by the play of experiences. The movie may be joy or sorrow, triumph or tragedy, but the screen is never stained.

This is the secret unity: experiencer and experience are one dance, one pulse, one vibration of the same mystery. To see this is to end the struggle of separation and to rest in the wholeness that has always been.

Think of music and hearing. Can you separate the two? Without hearing, music is no more than vibrations in the air. Without music, hearing has nothing to reveal. They arise together, dissolve together, like two lovers who never walk apart.

Or taste and the tongue. The tongue cannot taste without food, and food cannot be tasted without the tongue. The two are never truly apart; they are two ends of the same moment of experience.

Breath and life work the same way. You do not say, "First I lived, then I breathed." Nor, "First I breathed, then I lived." Life and breath are one event, one flow, one inseparable pulse.

So, it is with experiencer and experience. The mind splits them, "I am here, the world is there." But in truth, there is only one seamless happening: awareness knowing. The knower and the known are not-two. Just as fire and its warmth cannot be pulled apart, or a coin cannot have only one side, experiencer and experience cannot be pried into separate realities.

When this is seen, the whole game of separation softens. The world is no longer "out there" to be conquered or feared. It is a dance "in here," within awareness, inseparable from the one who witnesses it.

The Qualityless Presence

The experiencer is not an object. It cannot be described as "this" or "that." It has no form to outline, no color to point at, no weight to measure. It has no beginning, no ending, no location.

It cannot be placed in a box, for it is not "something" among other things. And yet, it is the ground of all things. It does not come or go. It cannot be limited, bound, or destroyed. It is timeless, indivisible, whole. To call these its "qualities" is misleading, for they are not attributes but reminders, reminders of what it is not. Whatever you can imagine or describe belongs to the realm of experience, not to the experiencer.

Here lies the paradox: that which cannot be known as an object is the most intimate fact of your being. The experiencer cannot be remembered and yet memory would not exist without it. It cannot be seen and yet it is the light of all seeing. It cannot be captured in thought and yet every thought sparkle within it.

The experiencer is not apart from you. It is you, not the "you" of body and personality, but the silent presence in which body, mind, and world appear and vanish. To seek it is futile, for the seeker itself is only a ripple within it. You will never "find" it, because you already are it.

It is existence itself, shining quietly as awareness. Always here. Always now. Always the background hum of being, unnoticed only because it is too close, too constant, too obvious. Like the space in which all things exist, it does not announce itself, but everything announces it. To recognize this is not to gain something new, but to fall into the simple intimacy of what has never left. The experiencer is not hidden. It is only overlooked.

Summary

Existence is filled with appearances, sounds, thoughts, sensations, memories. Yet beneath them all is the silent witness, the experiencer, pure awareness. The experiencer cannot be seen, touched, or remembered, because it is not an object. It is the very light by which all objects are known. Like the eye that sees but cannot see itself, awareness reveals everything but is never revealed as a "thing."

It shines by its own light, self-illumined, needing no proof. Even ignorance and sleep testify to its presence. Without it, no knowing would ever be possible.

Experiencer and experience arise together, inseparable like wave and water, flame and warmth, mirror and reflections. Awareness is never stained by what it reveals, joy and sorrow pass, but the witness remains untouched.

It has no qualities, no form, no place. And yet it is the most intimate fact of being, nearer than thought, nearer than "I am."

To realize this is not to gain something new, but to see what has always been true: You are not merely the appearances. You are not even the witness behind them.

You are the unbroken field in which both arise. The play of life continues, but the one who rests in this knowing is free.

Exercises: Meeting the Experiencer

1. Mirror Game

- Sit before a mirror.
- Look into your eyes. Ask gently: Who is looking?
- Notice: the one who looks cannot be seen. Rest there.

2. The Glove Trick

- Put on a glove. Move your fingers inside.
- Notice: the glove is not the hand.
- Just so, body and mind are not the experiencer.
- Remove the glove slowly, whispering: I am the one who wears all forms, but is never any form.

3. The Sun & Moon

- Step outside at night. Look at the moon.
- Remember: the moon shines only by the light of the sun.
- Close your eyes: All my experiences are moons. The experiencer is the sun that never needs another light.

4. Playful Pause

- Stop randomly during the day.
- Ask: Am I the action, or am I the one who knows the action?
- Smile. You just touched the experiencer.

Guided Meditation: Meeting the Experiencer

Step 1: Settle

Sit comfortably. Close your eyes.
Take a deep breath in... and out.
Let the body soften, as though it is a garment you are wearing.

Step 2: Notice Experience

Feel the body's weight.
The rhythm of your breath.
The sounds around you.
All of these are experiences, shifting, flowing.

Step 3: Notice Thoughts

Memories, images, words arise.
They appear and fade.
These too are experiences.

Step 4: Look Deeper

Ask: Who is noticing this?
Not the body. It is noticed.
Not the thought. It is noticed.
What is it that notices?

Step 5: Touch the Experiencer

It cannot be seen.
It cannot be touched.
And yet, you know it is here.
It is the silent space in which all appears.

Step 6: Playful Imagery

Imagine invisible glasses resting on your face.
You search everywhere for them,
But they were never missing.
The experiencer is like that, always present.

Step 7: Rest

Rest as that.
Not the thoughts, not the sensations, not the roles you play.
But the one to whom they appear.
Timeless, still, open.

Closing

Take one slow breath in... and out. Smile softly. Carry this awareness into your day, like a quiet companion always with you.

The experiencer is not something you gain. It is what you never lost. To rest here is to live as freedom itself.

Chapter 15

Practicing the Witness

Reflections, Meditations, and Mantras for Living Awareness

No edges, No borders.
No place to stand.
The experiencer is not a star
shining in some faraway sky,
but the vastness in which
all stars appear.
You cannot measure it,
for it has no length.
You cannot weigh it,
for it carries no mass.
You cannot find its shape,
for it is the shapeless womb
of all shapes.
Yet here it is, in your seeing,
in your breathing,
in your wondering.
Silent, Partless, Whole.

The screen behind the storm.
The stillness beneath the song.
The home you never left.

1. The witness is unseen, yet without it nothing can be seen.

Reflection:
Every sight, sound, and thought appears and disappears. Yet something remains, silently watching. The witness is not an object among objects; it is the open presence that holds them all. You cannot see it because it is the seer.

Practice:
Close your eyes. Notice sensations in the body, sounds around you, thoughts drifting. Now shift attention: who is aware of these? Rest not in the objects, but in the awareness holding them.

2. Experiencer and experience are one breath, not two.

Reflection:
Breath and breathing cannot be separated. So too, experiencer and experience rise together, inseparable. The division of "me here" and "world there" is only conceptual. In reality, it is one seamless happening.

Practice:
Follow your breath for a few moments. Notice how breath and

awareness arrive together, inseparable. Let go of the idea of "breather" and "breath." Just experience the one flow.

3. What you seek as truth is the seeker itself.

Reflection:
The journey looks outward: searching in scriptures, teachers, philosophies. But what you seek is not an object outside you. It is the light within you that makes seeking possible. The seeker and the sought are never two.

Practice:
Sit quietly and ask: "Who is seeking?" Instead of answering with words, turn attention back to the sense of "I." Rest in that awareness itself.

4. The eye cannot see itself, yet it illuminates the world.

Reflection:
The eye reveals mountains, rivers, stars and yet cannot turn to see itself. The witness, too, reveals everything but cannot be made into a thing. Its invisibility is not weakness but its greatest proof.

Practice:
Look around. Let the eyes rest on objects without naming them. Notice: the seer is present, but never visible. Let this recognition sink in. The unseen makes all else visible.

5. You are not the wave, nor even its watcher, you are the ocean.

Reflection:
Waves rise and fall, some calm, some violent. But the ocean is never reduced or enlarged by them. So too, thoughts and emotions dance, but the awareness in which they appear is vast, steady, untouched.

Practice:
When emotions rise, instead of identifying, ask: "Am I the wave, or is it rising in me?" Feel yourself as the ocean, wide and unmoved, letting waves come and go.

6. The experiencer has no qualities yet is the ground of all qualities.

Reflection:
It has no shape, no sound, no form. Yet every form shines in it. It is emptiness giving rise to fullness. Like space, it contains all yet remains untouched.

Practice:
Sit in silence. Whatever arises like sound, thought, sensation, whisper inwardly: "This too arises in awareness." Feel the openness that contains all without being altered.

7. The search ends where it began: in the light of awareness.

Reflection:
We chase knowledge, teachers, practices only to discover the

truth was always here. Awareness does not need to be attained, only recognized. The circle of seeking ends in stillness.

Practice:
Pause. Let go of all effort for just a moment. Do not search, do not strive. Simply rest in being. Notice: even without effort, awareness is already here.

8. Too near to grasp, too constant to notice, this is what you are.

Reflection:
The most obvious is the most overlooked. Like space, awareness is everywhere, yet unseen. Like glasses worn on the nose, it hides by being too close. This intimacy is your very nature.

Practice:
Whisper inwardly: "I am aware." Don't add anything else. Just rest in the simple fact of being aware. Nothing to hold, nothing to lose, simply this.

Playful Exercise: Meeting the Partless One

1. Close your eyes. Notice the space behind them.
2. Listen to sounds. They come and go. Yet something in you remains steady.
3. Ask: What shape does the experiencer have?

- (No shape appears.)

4. Ask: What color is it?
    - (Nothing shows up.)
5. Ask: Where is it? In your head? In your chest? Somewhere else?
    - (Wherever you look, you find only experiences, never the experiencer.)

Smile. That's the point. The experiencer is not an object at all. It is the open field in which everything is seen. Empty. Timeless. Partless. Perfect.

Practice: Mantras for Remembering the Experiencer

Sometimes words are not for analysis, but for rhythm, repetition, and play. These mantras are little doorways, choose whichever feels alive for you. Whisper it gently or let it echo inward like a song without a singer.

1. Poetic

"I am the sky; thoughts are nothing but passing clouds."
When storms of the mind swirl, let this mantra return you to vastness.

2. Playful

"Peekaboo! I see... and I am the seeing." Smile as you say it. Treat awareness like a child's game, simple, direct, light.

3. Minimalist

"I am." No frills. No concepts. Just pure presence. Soft, steady, like breath.

4. Devotional

"O Witness, you are my home." Let these words be a bow, an offering to the silent experiencer within and beyond.

Try these mantras throughout your day. Whisper them while sipping tea, waiting at a red light, or gazing at the stars. Each time, you'll notice: the experiencer is always here, unchanging, empty, blissful. The mantras do not point you somewhere else. They simply remind you: You are already home.

Chapter 16

The Dance of Experience

Dreamlike, fleeting, weightless
yet always shimmering on the screen of awareness

The river flows,
shapes rise and fall,
laughter echoes, tears glisten.
All pass like clouds.
Yet the sky remains
silent, wide, unbroken.
Rest, even for a moment,
as the sky,
watching the dance of passing clouds.

And yet, the movie continues. The experiencer abides still, silent, and untouched but the screen is never blank. It is always alive with appearances, that endless kaleidoscope we call experience. Sounds arrive and fade like visitors at a train station. Thoughts shimmer, dissolve, return, then vanish again into the unseen.

Emotions flare like fire, soften into embers, and dissolve into cool ash. Bodies move, grow, decay, transform. The experiencer is never disturbed. The show never pauses. Like music flowing out of silence, life keeps on singing.

Experience as Dream and Rainbow

Experiences feel so solid, so undeniable, so urgent. And yet their true nature is lighter than mist.

Like a Dream

At night, you dream. The dream-lover kisses you; the dream-monster terrifies you; the dream-rain soaks your skin. It feels real. But when you awaken, the whole drama evaporates in an instant. Not a single drop of that rain touched your bed.

Waking life is not so different. The same vividness, the same urgency and the same vanishing. What you swore was life-or-death yesterday is just a story today.

Like a Rainbow

A rainbow bends across the sky, dazzling, undeniable, irresistible. But try to touch it, and your hand comes back empty. Chase it, and it slips further away.

Experiences are just the same. Try to grasp joy, and it fades. Try to trap sorrow, and it shifts. Everything moves like light in the air. Beautiful, yes. Lasting, no.

The Cat and the Laser

A cat chases a red laser dot across the floor. Pounce! Leap! Skitter! The cat believes the dot is real. The faster it runs, the faster the dot escapes. But the dot is nothing by itself, it only exists because of light. We are like that cat.

Endlessly chasing experiences: pouncing on joy, resisting sorrow, grasping at success, clinging to comfort. But the wise one smiles, knowing the trick. The dot was never real. It was only light dancing.

The Nature of Experience

Impermanent.
No sound, thought, or feeling stays long enough to be grasped. The bird sings, and the song is gone before you finish listening. A thought sparkles like lightning, then melts into the night. Even pain, which feels endless when it burns, shifts into memory sooner than you realize. Everything flows, not one moment pauses for you to say, “Stay.” Experience is a river, never a stone.

Weightless.
Try holding on to yesterday’s laughter, where is it now? Try saving tomorrow’s tears in advance, can you? Experience leaves no footprints. You cannot carry joy in your pocket, nor tuck sorrow away in a drawer. By the time you say, “This is mine,” it is already gone. Experience is like perfume in the air, sweet while it lingers, but impossible to keep.

Dependent.
Nothing appears by itself. Every experience leans on a

thousand conditions: the body's state, the weather, the memory that flickers, the story you tell yourself, the world unfolding around you. Change even one thread, and the whole tapestry shifts. Anger may flare because of hunger. Joy may blossom because of sunlight. A memory may alter the taste of a moment. Experience is not born alone; it is a child of countless parents.

Empty.

Experiences seem so solid, so convincing. But look closely, where is their substance? A dream feels real until you wake up. A rainbow glows bright, yet no one has ever touched it. Experience too is vivid but hollow, a painting on water. It dazzles the senses, it stirs the heart, but when you try to grasp its core, your hands close on air.

And yet...

Though experiences are fleeting, insubstantial, and dependent, something steady is always here: the noticing. The sound fades, but the hearing remains. The thought dissolves, but the awareness of it lingers. The feeling passes, but the capacity to know does not pass. This noticing is the silent thread running through the whole tapestry of change. It does not age with the body, nor come and go with moods. It is the one constant, the groundless ground, the open space in which the impermanent dance of experience takes place.

To see this is freedom: you no longer cling to the shifting shapes of the river. You rest in the stillness of the shore, the silent witness, always present, always here.

Exercise: Watching the Flow of Change

1. Sit quietly. Close your eyes if you like. Let the world come to you.
2. Notice one thing, a sound, a sensation in the body, a thought.
3. Stay with it gently. Watch how it shifts, becomes louder or softer, pleasant or unpleasant, present or gone.
4. Now notice another thing, a new sound, sensation, or thought. See how this too arises, changes, and fades.
5. Ask softly:
    - "What in me noticed the change?"
    - "Is that noticing itself changing?"
6. Smile. You have just witnessed impermanence in action.

All experiences flow like a river. But the noticing, the silent, steady experiencer, remains still.

Closing Reflection

Experience is the dance, the play, the rainbow shimmer of life. It enchants, delights, and sometimes overwhelms. But just as a movie cannot appear without its screen, experience cannot exist without the experiencer. To see this is freedom: to enjoy the comedy, to weep at the tragedy, to marvel at the mystery, and yet to know, with quiet certainty, that the screen remains unbroken. The dance may whirl, but you are the stillness beneath its rhythm.

Chapter 17

The Tomato and the Dream

How Illusions Weave Themselves

The seeker sat beneath the shade of an old tree, eyes shimmering with curiosity, but also with doubt.

“Master,” he said hesitantly, “you keep telling me everything I experience is an illusion. But if that is so... who is weaving this illusion? And how can one illusion give birth to another?”

The master did not answer with words. Instead, he reached into a small basket at his side and pulled out a plump, ripe tomato. Turning it slowly in his palm, he asked,

“Tell me, what do you see?”

The seeker chuckled lightly, thinking it was a trick. “A tomato, of course.”

“And what makes it a tomato?” the master asked, eyes glinting.

The seeker leaned closer. “Its red skin, its roundness, its smoothness... and the smell, the taste I know it has.”

The master raised the tomato to the sunlight. “But look carefully. Are these qualities in tomato, or in you? The redness is not in the tomato; it is in your eyes. The smell is not in the tomato; it is in your nose. The smoothness is not in the tomato; it is in your touch. Without your senses, where is the tomato?” The seeker faltered. “Then... nothing remains?”

The master smiled, shaking his head gently. “Not nothing. Pure potential. An ocean of possibilities waiting to be shaped by your instruments of perception. The tomato is not an object ‘out there.’ It is a performance, created by your senses, interpreted by your mind.”

The seeker stared at the tomato as though seeing it for the first time.

The Trick of Memory

The master placed the tomato on the ground and asked, “When you close your eyes, where is it?”

The seeker closed his eyes. “It disappears,” he admitted.

“And yet,” the master said, “tomorrow you will say: ‘I saw a tomato yesterday.’ Who preserved the tomato for you?”

“My memory,” the seeker replied slowly.

“Exactly,” the master said with a grin. “Memory is the great magician. It takes fleeting shadows and pretends they are solid. Without memory, no world would persist. No time, no story, no you as you think yourself to be.”

The seeker lowered his gaze, his mind suddenly quiet.

One Dream, One Show

The master leaned in, voice soft and playful. "Now tell me, if objects are illusions, if senses are illusions, if memory itself is illusion, how can one illusion give rise to another?"

The seeker's brow furrowed in frustration.

The master laughed gently. "Have you ever dreamed of eating food in a dream kitchen, using dream utensils, with a dream stomach?"

"Yes," the seeker whispered.

"And did you not feel the food fill you, taste its flavors, believe it was real?"

The seeker's eyes widened.

"Exactly," the master said, tapping his arm. "The dream isn't happening to you. The dream is happening as you. Experience is one dream wearing countless masks.

The tomato, the senses, the memory, the thinker, all belong to the same show. But behind it all, you remain untouched. You are not in the dream; the dream is in you."

The Tomato Test (Playful Practice)

The master placed the tomato gently into the student's hand.

"Now," he said with a twinkle in his eye, "let us play a little game."

1. Look at the tomato. See its redness. Now close your eyes. Where is red?

2. Smell the tomato. Take in its aroma. Now stop smelling. Where is the aroma?

3. Touch the tomato. Feel its smooth skin. Now withdraw your hand. Where is the smoothness?

4. Finally, close your eyes and sit in silence. Ask yourself: If all qualities vanish when the senses rest, what is left? Who is here to notice their disappearance?

The student obeyed. Silence descended.

The master leaned closer and whispered, “That which remains is you, the experiencer. Not the tomato, not the senses, not even memory. You are the silent witness behind it all.”

The tomato was no longer just a tomato. It had become a doorway.

Moral of the Story

What you call “the world” is not outside of you. It is a play of senses and memory unfolding within you. Experience is not something happening to you, it is something happening as you.

Close your eyes.
The red of the tomato has vanished.
The smoothness has vanished.
The smell, the taste, gone.

Yet something remains.
Silent. Aware.

That which notices the vanishing
was never born
and can never vanish.

Rest there,
as the experiencer, untouched,
the open screen upon which
all flavors of life appear and disappear.

Chapter 18

The Essence in 20 Breaths

These practices complete the second step of the journey. To anchor the path, here is the essence, like 20 breaths of remembrance:

A Pocket Calendar of Awareness

Day 1 – Life is a Dream

Live today as both dreamer and dream.
Everything feels solid, yet ask softly:

"Is this any more real than last night's dream?"

Smile. Play along.

Day 2 – Separation is Imagination

When you meet someone, whisper inside:

"We are not two."

Feel the thread of oneness hidden beneath differences.

Day 3 – The Seeker is Hide and Seek

When you notice yourself searching, pause.

"Who is seeking?"

Then laugh, it is consciousness looking for itself.

Day 4 – Shadows and Substance

Worries and opinions feel heavy.

But ask: "Is this shadow... or substance?"

Let it lighten.

Day 5 – Not the Body, Not the Mind

Feel an itch, a joy, a thought.

Whisper: "This is happening in me, not to me."

Day 6 – All is Lila

Treat everything today as play.

Delay, mistake, success, surprise, all part of the game.

Smile like a child.

Day 7 – The Guru is a Mirror

When wisdom appears, don't cling to the teacher.
Ask: "What in me is being reflected now?"

Day 8 – Concepts Point, Experience Reveals

Take one teaching.

Don't repeat it. Live it.

"I am not the body", notice it as you breathe, eat, walk.

Day 9 – Maya's Costumes

Look at a flower, a car, a face.

Say inwardly: "This is nothingness dressed in colors."

Day 10 – Ego is a Shadow

When "I want, I know, I deserve" flares, pause.
Is it real? Or just a shadow on the wall?

Day 11 – Memory the Magician

Notice how quickly a moment vanishes.
The "movie" only runs because memory stitches the frames.

Day 12 – Liberation is Knowing

Don't try to become spiritual.
Whisper: "I already am."
That is enough.

Day 13 – Untouched Witness

Storms of thought may swirl.
But awareness is never stained.
The sky remains clear.

Day 14 – Awareness as Canvas

See today as a painting.
Sounds, colors, moods — brushstrokes.
The canvas — awareness — never leaves.

Day 15 – Emptiness is Potential

When something ends, don't mourn.
Notice: emptiness is not loss.
It is the womb of new beginnings.

Day 16 – The Still Witness

As sensations shift, ask:
"What changes? What doesn't?"
Abide as the unmoving witness.

Day 17 – Ripples of Perception

Touch a cup, a leaf, your own hand.
Ask: "Am I touching essence, or only ripples?"

Day 18 – Memory Creates Time

Notice past and future.
They live only as memory and imagination.
Right now is timeless.

Day 19 – Not Two

Close your eyes. Hear a sound.
Ask: "Is this sound separate from the hearing?"
Rest in the unity.

Day 20 – The Only Practice

Listen.
Contemplate.
Abide.
That is enough

Chapter 19

The Quiet Explosion

Peeling Away "I Am This" to Discover "I Am"

I wear a thousand masks.
Some laugh, some ache, some shine.
Each one feels like me,
until it slips.
The body whispers: "You are mine."
The mind shouts: "You are me."
The heart sighs: "You belong to this feeling."
Yet when I look closely,
they are all passing guests.
Who am I, then, when the masks dissolve?
Not the wave that rises,
not the foam that falls,
but the ocean itself, still, vast, boundless.
Not "I am this,"
not "I am that,"
but simply: I am.
Silence answers the question,
not with words,
but with presence.

Life is full of questions. Most of them are practical, everyday ones:

What's for dinner?
Where's my phone?
Will they like me?

Life is full of masks. The mask of the professional, the mask of the parent, the mask of the rebel, the mask of the lover. They glitter, they ache, they smile, they weep. And every time you wear one, you say: "Ah yes, this is me."

But wait. The moment it slips, another mask comes. Which one is the real you? The body says, "I am you." But scratch your skin and even the cells betray you, they die, renew, vanish. Which of those trillions was the "real" you?

The mind shouts, "I am you." But watch closely: thoughts tumble like monkeys on caffeine. Today's truth becomes tomorrow's lie. Are you really that circus? The heart sighs, "You are this feeling." But feelings are like the weather, stormy in the morning, sunny in the afternoon, cloudy by night. If you are feeling, then who are you when the feeling leaves?

One by one, the masks fall. And then the great joke of existence dawns: You were never the mask. You were never even the face behind the mask. You were the space in which mask and face appeared.

Why Bother Asking?

You could live your whole life without ever touching this question. Millions do. They wake up, brush their teeth, rush to work, scroll through their phones, fall in love, fight, laugh, cry, chase promotions, collect possessions, grow old, and one day: poof - disappear. The play goes on, perfectly complete in its own way.

And yet... every so often, the script falters. The curtain twitches. The stage set creaks. Suddenly, the solid ground of "this is who I am" starts trembling.

The body, so proudly claimed as me, reveals its fragility with one visit to the doctor, one surprising pain, one gray hair.

The mind, so confidently taken as I, turns into a hall of mirrors, contradicting itself, spinning in circles, forgetting what it just said.

The identity built on achievements and possessions, the glittering "this is my worth," collapses overnight when a job is lost, a relationship ends, or fortune turns its face away.

It is in these cracks that the question sneaks in. Softly, playfully, like a mischievous child tugging at your sleeve:

"Yes, yes, you have all these roles. But when the costumes fall off, who are you really?"

This question is not polite. It does not wait for the right time. It ambushes you when you are least prepared: in the hospital bed, in the silence after heartbreak, in the middle of a sleepless night. And sometimes, even in moments of joy, it whispers behind the laughter: Who is the one laughing?

You may try to hush it with distractions, scrolling, shopping, and entertainment. You may bury it under philosophy, religion, or psychology. But the question is patient. It does not go away.

It waits like a seed beneath the soil, ready to sprout the moment a little rain of awareness touches it.

And when it sprouts, it changes everything. Because it is not an ordinary question. It is dynamite hidden in three small words:

Who am I?

Asked once, casually, it passes like a breeze. Asked deeply, with sincerity, it shakes the very roots of your being. Because this question doesn't want an answer in words. It wants an answer in silence. It doesn't want concepts; it wants truth.

This is why the sages bothered. Why mystics laughed. Why did seekers across ages risk everything for it. Because once asked sincerely, the question doesn't just point to who you are, it dissolves everything you are not.

Peeling the Onion

The sages gave us a simple game, almost childlike in its daring:

Peel. Peel. Peel.

Start with the obvious:

This body, oh yes, so convincing! But look closer. It has already changed a thousand times. The baby's skin, the teenager's swagger, the adult's lines, the elder's stoop.

Which one is you? Which one lasted? Peel.

Then emotions: joy bubbling, sorrow dripping, anger flashing, love glowing. Each feels like the whole truth when it comes. But none of them stay. They're like actors barging on stage, giving their performance, bowing out. Peel.

Thoughts? Ah, the noisy tenants of the mind. They argue, contradict, pretend to be wise. But look each thought vanishes before you can even hold it. Peel.

Memories? Tricksters! They edit themselves without asking permission, turning villains into heroes and failures into comic relief. Yesterday itself looks different today.

Peel.

And then suddenly you're left holding... nothing.

But here is the cosmic punchline: this "nothing" is not the bleak emptiness of a grave. It is the luminous emptiness of the sky. Open, boundless, alive. The kind of emptiness from which birds fly, clouds drift, stars burn, and galaxies whirl.

That "nothing" is actually the very space in which everything happens. It is so generous that it allows every passing mask, every fleeting wave, every fleeting story to appear and dissolve without complaint.

This is why the sages laughed. They knew the joke. The search ends not with some solid "thing" called truth, but with the discovery that the truth is spaciousness itself, an emptiness so full that the whole universe dances inside it.

From "I Am This" to Just "I Am"

So here you are, having peeled body, mind, memory, story, left with nothing. And at first it feels strange, even unsettling. We are so used to being something, a role, a name, a history that “nothing” sounds like loss. But stay a little longer in this vast openness.

Notice: though everything has been peeled away, you have not vanished.

Something remains.

What is it?

Not a “thing” at all, but a shining, silent fact: I am.

Not “I am tall.”

Not “I am sad.”

Not “I am successful.”

Those are costumes, props, shadows.

Just... I am.

This is the seed-truth before the story grows. The naked flame before it becomes smoke and firewood and ash. The clear sky before clouds write their poetry across it.

When you rest here, something subtle shifts:

- The body may ache, but you are not the ache.
- Thoughts may race, but you are not the noise.
- Emotions may roar, but you are not swept away.

You are the witness in which they appear and vanish. You are the silent screen upon which the whole movie plays.

You have always been this. You never became the witness; you only mistook yourself for the passing actors on the stage.

The onion has no solid core to grab, only this luminous spaciousness that says: I am. And in that simple, unadorned beingness, the whole universe rises and falls like waves in an ocean that was never disturbed.

The Trick of "Mine"

Language gives us away.

We say: my body, my thoughts, my feelings, my ideas, my past, my future.

But pause for a moment. If it is mine, it cannot be me.

You lose your house, yet you remain.

You lose your hair, yet you remain.

You even forget your memories and still something remains to say, "I don't remember."

That something is the silent constant, the one who owns without being owned, who holds without being held.

Watch closely and the trick reveals itself: the body changes, thoughts spin, emotions rise and crash like waves on a shore. All of them wear the costume of mine, but no one can claim the throne of me.

The witness does not age when the body ages. The witness does not drown when the mind floods with thought. The witness does not vanish when memory goes silent. It is always there, a background hum, quiet and unwavering.

The sages called it sakṣhi : the seer, the experiencer, the one that never moves even while the whole universe plays musical chairs.

And here is the playful punchline: You spend a lifetime polishing the chairs, decorating them, defending them, while the one who is actually sitting was never touched at all.

The Quiet Explosion

And then, without warning, the cosmic prank lands.

All the labels you've been collecting, body, mind, emotions, history, slip through your fingers.

You realize, not as an idea but as a shock of clarity:
You are not the body.
You are not the mind.
You are not the emotions.
You are not even the carefully narrated story of your life.
You are awareness itself.

No trumpets sound, no lightning bolts fall from the sky. Instead, a gentle, quiet explosion takes place inside you. An inner demolition of illusion. The walls you thought were so solid, "I am this," "I am that", suddenly reveal themselves as cardboard props.

And in that moment, everything flips. Or perhaps, for the first time, everything is finally right-side up.

You see with dazzling simplicity:

I am not in existence. I am existence.

The long search collapses. The seeker and the sought dissolve into the same space. The one chasing and the one being chased were never two.

And then?

Life continues, beautifully ordinary. You eat breakfast, answer emails, argue with your neighbor, laugh at a joke. The masks still dance. The play still unfolds. But something essential has changed: you no longer mistake yourself for the mask.

You wear roles lightly now, joyfully, like costumes at a festival. You laugh at comedies, you cry at tragedies, but deep inside you know the secret. Behind every role, every costume, every drama that you are the stage itself.

Unmoving, silent, infinite.

Pure freedom is to play without clinging, to live without fear, to be without becoming.

The Quiet Explosion: A Meditation

Step 1: Settle
Sit quietly.
Let your body rest.
Take a deep breath in... and let it go.
Again.
One more time.
Now let the breath move naturally, without effort.

Step 2: Notice the Body
Bring attention to the body.
Notice its weight on the chair, the floor beneath you.
This body has changed since birth.

It keeps changing, cells dying, cells renewing.
If it changes... can it be you?

Whisper inside: Not this.

Step 3: Notice the Mind
Now watch the mind.
Thoughts come and go, like clouds across a sky.
One moment happy, the next restless.
They rise and vanish, never still.
If they change... can they, be you?

Whisper inside: Not this.

Step 4: Notice the Emotions
Now touch the heart.
Feeling's ripple joy, sorrow, calm, longing.
Each has its season. Each dissolves.
If they come and go... can they, be you?

Whisper inside: Not this.

Step 5: Notice the Memories
Now recall a memory.
Perhaps of childhood, or yesterday.
Notice how it appears like a picture in the mind.
Memories change, fade, vanish.
If they shift and break... can they be you?

Whisper inside: Not this.

Step 6: What Remains?
Body, mind, emotions, memories...
All passing guests.
So who is the host?
What remains when all else is set aside?

Listen.
Notice the silent space in which everything appears.
This clear, shining awareness.
Unmoved. Untouched. Unchanging.

Step 7: The Quiet Explosion
Here the secret reveals itself:
You are not the body.
You are not the mind.
You are not the emotions.
You are not the story.

You are awareness itself.

Closer than breath.
Closer than thought.
Always here.

This is the quiet explosion; gentle, vast, total.

8: Rest in Being
Do nothing now.
No effort.
Just rest as the witness.
The play of life continues, thoughts, sounds, sensations.
But you remain the stage upon which they dance.

You are not in existence.
You are existence.

Stay here... for a few breaths.
Rest in this presence.
Silent. Open. Whole.

End with a gentle smile.

Chapter 20

Life Without the Doer

Freedom in the Simplicity of Being

I searched for "me" in the mirror,
but only found reflections.
I searched for "me" in my thoughts,
but they shifted like sand.
I searched for "me" in my body,
but it aged, changed, slipped away.
At last, in the silence between breaths,
I discovered,
there is no "I" to be found.
And yet, awareness shines.
Unbroken. Untouched. Unnamed.
Like the sky, it owns no clouds,
yet without it, clouds cannot drift.
Like space, it holds all,
yet itself remains unseen.
To live as this is simple freedom:
not escape from life,
but resting as the vastness
in which life dances.

At some point, every seeker stumbles upon a discovery so disarmingly simple that it feels almost absurd:

There is no "I."

The "I" that you defend with arguments, decorate with achievements, dramatize with stories, is nothing but a label, a name written on water. Remove the label, and nothing is lost. The jar remains when the sticker is peeled away. Life continues when the mask is removed. And what shines forth is not absence, but presence itself, awareness, pure, simple, luminous.

Life Without the Doer

At first, this realization seems impossible. If there is no "I," then who eats, who works, who loves? But when it lands, the discovery is liberating. It does not destroy life. It lightens it.

You suddenly see:

- I am not the doer. Actions flow through this body like wind moving through bamboo, hollow, effortless, resonant.
- I am not the owner. Nothing belongs to me because everything already belongs to the whole. The river does not "own" its waters; it simply flows.
- I am not even a "someone." The separate identity dissolves into something vaster, leaving only the clear witness, the silent background in which life happens.

This is not renunciation. You don't need to throw away your clothes or run to the Himalayas. This is relief. You realize that nothing was ever yours to drop. Life continues eating, walking, working, laughing, loving. But the tight knot of "my success, my failure, my story" loosens into a quiet smile.

A Strange Kind of Ownership

Imagine this: if the whole sky were yours, would you still fight for a single cloud? When the idea of self dissolves, life becomes strangely intimate. Everything is yours because nothing is yours. The flowers by the road, the stranger's laughter, the sunset beyond the city, all belong, yet none are "owned."

This detachment is not cold indifference. It is warmth without possession. Love without chains. You feel sorrow, but you don't drown in it. You taste joy, but you don't chase after it. Life flows through you fully, but lightly, like the fragrance of jasmine drifting in the night air.

Fearless Living

As this insight deepens, fear begins to wither.
How can existence be afraid of existence?

Petty worries shrink into shadows, money, reputation, possessions, once so large, now seen as toys on a child's carpet. You still live in the world, but the weight of the world no longer rests on your shoulders.

Discovering awareness is like discovering that the small puddle you were guarding is actually the ocean itself. Once you know this, the little splashes on the shore no longer disturb you.

This is not apathy. It is clarity.

- Greed looks like a child clutching marbles.
- Anger looks like a tantrum in the sandbox.
- Jealousy looks like shadow-puppets dancing on a wall.

They may still appear, but you do not climb into their game. You watch, you smile, you let them pass.

Awareness as Abiding

So, what now? What should you “do” with this discovery? The most surprising answer: nothing at all. Abiding means resting in what is already here. Like a river resting in its own flow. Like the sky resting in its own openness.

- I am not this body. The body comes and goes.
- I am not this thought. Thoughts flicker and vanish.
- I am not this mood. Emotions roll in and roll out like clouds.
- I am the witness, steady, silent, luminous.

Sometimes you’ll forget. You’ll get caught up again in the drama of “me and mine.” That’s okay. Just notice. Smile at your own forgetfulness. Return gently, as if waking from a daydream with a chuckle. Awareness never left. It was only overlooked.

You don't need to force it. No endless rituals, no acrobatics of meditation, no striving. Awareness is not a destination, it is what has always been here, waiting to be noticed.

The Simplicity of It All

Self-realization is not a firecracker show. The body does not vanish into light. The world does not flip upside down. Angels do not start singing in your ears.

The miracle is far quieter: you are seeing changes. That's all. But that is enough.

Once you know yourself as awareness, life ceases to be a burden. It becomes a dance, a game, a play. The sky does not stop storms, but it is never stained by them. So too, you remain untouched even as joys and sorrows move across your surface.

This is the freedom you have always had, hidden beneath the story of "I." Not freedom from life, but freedom in life.

Playful Meditation: "The Sky of Me"

Try this today:

1. Close your eyes. Notice your thoughts as they pass.
2. Imagine each thought as a cloud, dark, fluffy, lightning streaked.
3. Ask gently: What is the sky in which these clouds appear? That sky is your true nature, vast, silent, untouched.

4. Sit for a minute, smiling at the clouds. Watch them dance. Let them go.

5. Whisper to yourself: I am the sky, not the clouds.

Extra Contemplations for Daily Life

- **When angry:** Ask, “Is this cloud me, or am I the sky?”
- **When joyful:** Ask, “Can I enjoy this rainbow without needing it to last?”
- **When lost:** Whisper, “The experiencer is never lost.”

Chapter 21

Three Gentle Doors

Listening, Contemplation, and Abiding

You have completed step two of the journey. Naturally, questions arise: What now? How do I apply this knowledge? The answer is beautifully simple. On this path there are only three practices:

1. Listening
2. Contemplation
3. Abiding in the truth

Nothing more is required.

There is no need for rituals, austerities, or elaborate disciplines. The greatest achievement is knowledge itself, for you are already whole, already complete. Life is but a passing dream, a play upon the stage of awareness. The practice is not to change it, but to recognize it for what it is — an appearance within you. The essential task is to remain in knowledge, to remember the truth again and again, until it shines by itself.

1. Listening: Planting the Seed

Listening (śravaṇa) is the first and most essential step. It may seem simple, but true listening is rare.

To listen here is not to collect ideas or memorize words. It is to open fully, mind, heart, and being, to the teaching. When you listen deeply, you allow the words of truth to sink beneath the surface of thought, like rain seeping into thirsty soil.

You may need to revisit certain passages, hearing them again and again until their meaning becomes clear. This is natural. Listening is not about speed but depth. Avoid mixing teachings from many streams, for that only clouds the waters. Drink deeply from one source until clarity dawns.

Use the language of the path as it is given. Words matter. They carry precision born of centuries of inquiry. Let them become part of your vocabulary, not for their own sake, but because they keep your understanding sharp and your communication with your teacher and fellow seekers clear.

Listening plants, the seed of wisdom. Without it, no further growth is possible.

2. Contemplation: Nurturing the Seed

Once the words are heard, the mind naturally begins to stir. Doubts arise, questions form, and the intellect seeks to test what it has received. This is not resistance; it is the next step. Contemplation (manana) is the nurturing of the seed, ensuring it takes root.

Contemplation means verifying the truth for yourself. Ask: Does this teaching align with my experience? Does it make sense in the light of reason? Truth is never against reason; it only asks that reason be clear and free of bias.

Set aside time each day, an hour or two in silence, to reflect. Write down your thoughts, your doubts, your insights. Call upon the gurufield, the living essence of the teaching lineage, for support. This is not superstition but remembrance that you are part of a stream of seekers and teachers that flows beyond time.

Engage in dialogue, when possible, but avoid debate. To win an argument is to lose the spirit of inquiry. Let your conversations be questions and answers, not contests of victory. Use quizzes, self-reflection, or satsang to test and refine your understanding.

Over time, contemplation becomes second nature. The teachings move from being external ideas to inner certainties. The seed sprouts: green shoots appear. What was once heard as words is now known as truth.

3. Abiding: The Flowering of the Seed

When listening and contemplation have done their work, the knowledge begins to settle. Abiding (nididhyāsana) is the flowering of the seed into living realization.

Abiding is not effortful concentration. It is not the mechanical repetition of a phrase. It is the simple, natural resting in truth you have already seen. I am the awareness itself.

At first, you may forget. Old patterns and habits of identification will return. This is not failure. Abiding is the gentle art of returning, again and again, until remembrance becomes steady. Eventually, the truth shines on its own, without effort.

If the teaching feels dry or distant, it means it has not yet taken root. If conviction falters, purification may be needed to clear away inner obstructions. But know this: once the seed has sprouted, it cannot die. Sooner or later, it flowers.

As abiding deepens, peace arises naturally. Happiness and fulfillment no longer depend on outer circumstances. You do not become extraordinary; you discover the simplicity of being what you always were.

The flower does not strain to bloom; it opens because it must. So too, when the truth is ripened within, it expresses itself without effort.

One Current, Three Movements

Listening, contemplation, and abiding are not separate stages, but movements of a single current.

- Listening - plants the seed.
- Contemplation - nourishes it.
- Abiding - lets it flower.

The river flows into the ocean, and the ocean reveals it was never separate from the river.

And yet, remember: the truth is not postponed. It is available here and now. If readiness is complete, realization can dawn in an instant. Still, for most, the mind requires this refinement, hearing, reflecting, resting, until the obvious becomes undeniable.

In the end, what began as practice dissolves into presence. What began as effort dissolves into simplicity? The seeker disappears into the sought. The seed, the soil, the flower, all dissolve into the light of awareness.

Listen with openness.

Contemplate with clarity.

Abide with simplicity.

This is the whole path.

Exercises for Listening (Śravaṇa)

1. **Focused Re-Reading:**

- Choose one short passage from the teaching.
- Read it slowly three times.
- After the third reading, close your eyes and recall it in your own words.
- Notice: Did you only remember the words, or did you grasp the meaning?

2. **Silent Absorption:**

- Sit quietly and imagine the teaching being spoken directly to you by a living master.
- Let each phrase enter you like drops of water on parched soil.
- Do not rush to agree or disagree; just let the words rest inside.

3. **Vocabulary of Truth:**

- Write down key terms (e.g., awareness, Self, illusion, truth).
- Reflect on what each means in this path, not in common speech.
- Revisit them often until they feel natural in your language and thinking.

Exercises for Contemplation (Manana)

1. **Daily Reflection Journal:**

- Set aside 20–30 minutes in a quiet space.
- Pick one teaching (e.g., I am awareness, not the body).
- Write your thoughts, doubts, and logical reflections.
- End by noting one insight or clarity gained.

2. **Question & Answer with Yourself:**

- Write down a question your mind raises about the teaching.
- Then, write the answer as if your inner teacher were speaking.
- Compare: does the answer satisfy your reason and experience?

3. **Logic Test:**

- Take a common assumption (e.g., I am this body).
- Ask systematically: Can this always be true? Is it permanent? Does it fit my experience?

- Follow the inquiry until the false belief loosens.

Exercises for Abiding (Nididhyāsana)

1. **Returning to Awareness:**

- Several times a day, pause.
- Ask: Who is experiencing this moment?
- Rest, even for a few seconds, in the sense of "I am awareness."

2. **Effortless Resting:**

- Sit quietly for 10 minutes without trying to control the mind.
- Whatever thought arises, notice it and let it pass, returning gently to the recognition: I am the witness.

3. **Carrying Knowledge into Life:**

- Choose one daily activity (walking, eating, conversing).
- While doing it, silently remind yourself: This too is appearing in me, the awareness.
- Let this remembrance soften and simplify the act.

These exercises are not mechanical drills but invitations to deepen what you already know. Use them gently. They are meant to support, not replace, the natural unfolding of understanding.

Chapter 22

Self-Evaluation of the Path

"The traveler pauses and asks: Am I moving toward the mountain, or am I wandering in circles? The mountain itself does not move, but the path may twist endlessly. How then do I know where I stand?"

At some point, every seeker confronts this question: Am I on the right path? Am I progressing or standing still? What are the signs of true growth, and what are the obstacles that hold me back?

Unlike a worldly journey, the inner path carries no milestones, no road signs, no visible distance markers. It is a silent unfolding. No bell rings to announce advancement. No outer authority can certify realization. This uncertainty often fills the seeker with restlessness.

Teachers often reassure: If your peace of mind, happiness, freedom, and sense of lightness steadily increase, you are walking in the right direction. Continue.

This simple criterion is true and sufficient for many. But some seekers feel a deeper thirst. They want clarity, nuance, even a subtle yardstick by which to measure themselves. And so, the exploration of self-evaluation arises.

The Paradox of Progress

Here lies the first paradox: the Self, the true "I", never progresses. It is already what it is: whole, perfect, unchanging. Awareness itself does not evolve, for it is timeless. To say that the Self moves would be like saying the sky travels when clouds drift across it.

What evolves is not awareness, but the layered structure of mind and memory, the body-mind complex. Over lifetimes, impressions condense into these layers, forming patterns of behavior, desires, fears, and identities. These are what shift and refine themselves. That movement is what we call progress.

When we say, "I am progressing," what we truly mean is: "The instrument through which I appear is becoming more refined." The Self shines regardless, but a dirty mirror scatters the light. Polishing the mirror does not improve the sun, it only allows its brilliance to be seen.

Thus, the wise seeker remembers, I, the Self, do not progress. Yet this illusion of a seeker evolves. It is within this play of illusion that self-evaluation becomes meaningful.

Why Self-Evaluation Matters

Without reflection, the seeker may wander in circles. A practice repeated without awareness can become a habit, not growth.

Rituals can become empty shells. Words of wisdom can become mere slogans. Without discernment, one risks confusing comfort for freedom.

Self-evaluation functions like a compass. It helps us ask: Is this practice bringing me more clarity, or only routine? Are afflictions loosening, or merely hiding beneath polite masks? Am I becoming lighter, or am I secretly building new chains under spiritual names?

It also allows course correction. Just as a sailor checks the stars to avoid drifting off course, the seeker examines their journey. Sometimes a practice no longer serves. Sometimes a teacher's method does not fit one's temperament. Sometimes laziness pretends to be acceptance, or stubbornness hides under loyalty. Self-evaluation shines light on these blind spots.

It keeps inquiry alive. Many seekers stop not because the truth is unreachable, but because they stop questioning themselves. They settle into a comfortable rhythm and mistake it for liberation. Self-evaluation shakes off this stagnation, clearing the dust before it hardens into rust.

The Instinct to Judge Others

Evaluation is not only inward. Humans are wired to evaluate others. Within seconds, the mind takes stock: Is this person a threat or a friend? Trustworthy or not? Attractive or unsuitable? These snap judgments are ancient survival tools.

Even today, we unconsciously assess others by their dress, tone, posture, and words. Scientific studies show how quickly impressions are formed sometimes in less than three seconds.

A decision is made before we consciously realize it, and the mind merely obeys what the deeper program has already decided.

For seekers, this instinct can be refined into conscious observation. One can notice patterns in another's speech, thought, or behavior and sense their level of maturity. But here lies danger. Knowledge can tempt the ego into manipulation or superiority. To misuse the ability to evaluate others is to fall into arrogance, the very opposite of what the path requires.

The guiding principle is simple: evaluate others lightly, yourself deeply. Use discernment with compassion, and only when asked. Otherwise, let others walk their path as you walk yours, remembering that the same essence dwells in all.

The Fragile Nature of Judgment

Evaluation is provisional. The mind is fluid, shifting daily and hourly. A joyful seeker in the morning may be restless by evening. A single event, a loss, a love, a new teaching can transform someone overnight. To freeze them in one judgment is to deny the river its flow.

Even long-term tendencies cannot be treated as absolute truth. Evaluation is useful for guidance, not for final verdicts. Held lightly, it illuminates; clutched tightly, it deceives.

Nor is self-evaluation a substitute for healing. It may reveal afflictions, but it cannot by itself resolve deep wounds. When necessary, humility demands that we seek guidance from teachers, mentors, or healers. Self-evaluation shows imbalance; other forms of support may be needed to restore harmony.

The Balance of Layers

How then can progress be recognized? By observing the balance of the inner layers. The human mind is not one thing, but many. It is a layered structure, built from countless impressions. Lower layers govern survival, desire, fear, and compulsion. Higher layers reveal compassion, creativity, discernment, and silence.

All layers are necessary. To despise the lower is ignorance; to idolize the higher is imbalance. True evolution lies in harmony, where the higher guide and the lower serve. An evolved seeker is not one who has destroyed the lower, but one who allows each layer to play its part in balance. Like an orchestra, all instruments remain, but the music shifts from noise to harmony.

Practical Signs in Daily Life

Because the layers themselves are invisible, they must be read through outer expression. Six signs offer practical mirrors:

Behavior – Actions become less reactive, more deliberate.

Speech – Words soften, becoming clearer and kinder.

Thought – Mental noise decreases, creativity and reflection increase.

Relationships – Shift from dependency and control to respect and freedom.

Entertainment – A movement away from crude distraction toward subtler joys.

Afflictions – Anger, pride, jealousy still arise but dissolve quickly, leaving no residue.

These parameters are not meant for boasting but for honest reflection. The ego loves to collect "proofs" of progress. But the true purpose is to see where light is entering and where shadows remain.

The Dynamics of Change

The layers are in constant motion. Within a single day, moods rise and fall. Over years, life reshapes priorities. A new book, a teacher's glance, a sudden heartbreak, any of these can shift the balance overnight. Even across lifetimes, old tendencies resurface, shaping talents and struggles. What seems sudden is often the ripening of ancient seeds. What feels stubborn may be the weight of many births. Progress, then, is not a fixed badge but a flowing process. Evaluation must respect this fluidity. It is the river's direction, not the ripples on its surface, that matters.

The Ordinary as Mirror

Ultimately, the measure of evolution is not found in mystical visions or rare experiences, but in the ordinariness of life.

- Are you calmer in traffic than you once were?

- Do your words wound less and heal more?
- Do you recover more quickly from anger or grief?
- Do you seek quieter joys rather than louder distractions?
- Do you sense freedom where once you felt bondage?

These ordinary shifts are the true signs of progress. They are small but profound. They show that life itself has become the mirror of practice.

The Final Reminder

Self-evaluation is a valuable tool. It prevents waste, encourages honesty, and fosters balance. But it belongs to the relative path, not the ultimate. The Self, the true “I, remains untouched, perfect, whole, free.

Evaluation is like a ladder. It helps the seeker climb, step by step. But once the roof is reached, the ladder is no longer needed. In realization, the very question of progress dissolves.

For behind all progress, beyond all evaluation, you are already what you seek, pure awareness, timeless and complete.

Thus, the art of self-evaluation is a lamp for the journey. Use it with humility. Let it guide you gently. And when dawn comes, even the lamp will no longer be needed, for the sun that was always shining will be seen in its full brilliance.

Practices for Self-Evaluation

To move from concept to direct experience, here are a few gentle practices you can weave into your journey. These are not rigid rules but invitations and tools for honest reflection without self-judgment.

1. Daily Mirror of Behavior

At the end of each day, sit quietly for a few minutes. Ask yourself:

- Were my actions today guided by impulse or by clarity?
- Did I act out of fear, anger, or greed? Or out of calmness and understanding?

Do not condemn yourself. Simply notice. Over time, patterns will reveal themselves.

2. Listening to Speech

During conversations, become aware of your words. Later, reflect:

- Were my words kind or careless?
- Did they heal or wound?
- Did I speak truth, or did I shade it for comfort or approval?

Speech is a living measure of your inner balance.

3. Journaling Thoughts

Each morning or evening, write down a few thoughts that have been repeating in your mind. Then ask:

- Are these thoughts constructive or compulsive?
- Do they nourish or drain me?
- Do they come from fear, or from love and clarity?

By journaling, you turn the vague stream of thought into something visible. Awareness itself begins to transform them.

4. Relationship Reflection

Think of three interactions you had today—with family, friends, or colleagues. Ask:

- Did I relate with respect or with possession?
- Did I give freedom, or try to control?
- Did I listen fully, or only wait to reply?

Relationships are mirrors—often sharper than solitude.

5. Entertainment as Teacher

Look honestly at how you have entertained yourself this week like movies, music, books, social media. Ask:

- Do these leave me restless or peaceful?
- Do they numb me or awaken me?

Entertainment reveals the taste of the mind. Over time, the seeker naturally gravitates toward subtler joys.

6. Observing Afflictions

When anger, jealousy, or pride arises, do not suppress it. Instead, notice:

- How long did they last?
- Did they control my actions, or dissolve quickly?
- Could I see them as passing clouds, or was I swept away?

This is perhaps the clearest indicator of progress: not the absence of afflictions, but their decreasing grip.

7. Weekly Self-Check

Once a week, sit in silence for 15 minutes. Ask simply:

- Am I lighter than last week?
- Am I freer than last year?
- What has softened? What still binds?

Do not seek perfection. Look for directions. Progress is measured not in leaps but in the steady trend toward balance and freedom.

8. The Teacher Within

Finally, ask: If I were my own teacher, what would I advise myself now? This shifts perspective, helping you see blind spots and next steps with clarity.

Closing

These practices are not to create self-judgment but self-clarity. They help you see the river's flow without clinging to any wave. Over time, you will notice that actions become calmer, speech softer, thoughts freer, relationships deeper, and afflictions lighter.

And yet, always remember, these are tools, not the truth itself. They guide within the dream, but the Self, the pure awareness that observes all, remains untouched, timeless, and whole.

Use the lamp of self-evaluation with care and humility, until the day dawns when the lamp is no longer needed and you see that you were always the light itself.

The Last Wordless Word

Now that you know it's a play:

Play fully
Sit for a moment.
Close this book.
The words have played their part,
like waves rising, cresting, dissolving.
But the ocean was always here.
Truth does not end in ink,
nor begin in pages.
It waits where silence waits,
where breath softens,
where you simply are.
Forget the seeker.
Forget the found.
Forget even forgetting.
Just rest.
The sky does not try to hold its clouds.
You need not hold yourself.
Look, already,
You are free.

Life is a dream, yet you are not caught in it, you are the awareness in which the dream unfolds. To see this is to live lightly, to laugh more easily, to let joy and sorrow come and go like clouds across the sky. Nothing needs to be achieved.

Nothing needs to be escaped. You are already whole, already home.

In the end, there is no end. The journey dissolves into the very ground upon which it was walked. The seeker disappears into the sought, and the questions dissolve into the silence from which they first arose. What remains is not a conclusion, but a clarity: simple, unadorned, eternal.

Emptiness is not barren. It shines. It is the light by which every form appears and the silence in which every sound resounds. It is the space that allows life to dance and the stillness that receives every step. To call it emptiness is to speak from the mind. To live it is to know its fullness, radiant, alive, without boundary.

There is nothing to attain, nothing to guard, nothing to lose. The self you believed yourself to be was never more than a passing shadow upon the vast sky of awareness. The sky remains. Infinite. Untouched. Free.

May these words not be taken as teachings, but as reminders.

May they return you, again and again, to the simplicity of being. To the immediacy of this breath. To the eternal presence in which all arises and subsides.

And when even these reminders fade, let the radiance of emptiness shine by itself, without guru, without seeker, without book.

In that shine, you are already home.

References & Inspirations:

This book stands in a long lineage of wisdom, a stream flowing through centuries of seekers, teachers, poets, and philosophers. While the words here are freshly woven, their fragrance comes from countless blossoms of thought and silence.

- Upanishads – The timeless revelations of non-duality.
- Shrimad Bhagavad Gita – Dialogue between Arjuna and Krishna, a perennial guide to the inner battle and liberation.
- Adi Śaṅkarācārya and the Advaita lineage for establishing clarity and precision in the path of knowledge.
- Ramana Maharshi for distilling the inquiry into a single, luminous question: Who am I?
- Eckhart Tolle, Mooji, Rupert Spira for modern voices echoing the ageless call to presence.
- Osho for bringing fire, laughter, and paradox to the path, awakening the heart to both love and emptiness.
- Tarun Pradhaan for being a living presence of guidance, clarity, and compassion, whose teachings on knowledge and awareness have been a direct inspiration for these writings.